Published by Little Toller Books in 2023

Text © William Henry Searle 2023

The right of William Henry Searle to be identified as the author
of this work has been asserted by him in accordance with the
Copyright, Design and Patents Act 1988

Jacket illustration © Holly Ovenden 2023

Typeset in Caslon by Little Toller Books

Printed in Cornwall by TJ Books

All papers used by Little Toller Books are natural, recyclable products
made from wood grown in sustainable, well-managed forests

A catalogue record for this book is available from the British Library

ISBN 978-1-908213-19-4

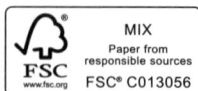

FSC
www.fsc.org

MIX
Paper from
responsible sources
FSC® C013056

ELOWEN

a story of grief and love

WILLIAM HENRY SEARLE

LITTLE TOLLER BOOKS

Contents

For Amy

The Dusk drew earlier in –
The Morning foreign shone –
A courteous, yet harrowing Grace,
As Guest, that would be gone –
And thus without a Wing
Or service of a Keel
Our Summer made her light escape
Into the Beautiful.

Emily Dickinson
from 'As Imperceptibly as Grief'

Prologue

The wind drops, the air sits heavy in my lungs.

Fog caps the ridge of the broad green hill that is Martin Down. A chalk path, lining the top of an earthwork ditch like a flattened furrow, ends abruptly in long, green grass. I hold the gate open for Amy, Mum, then Dad who is on his knees, then upright, then down again. He can't decide, in his haste to keep up, when is a good time to properly tie his bootlaces. He also drops his car keys. He is in so many minds.

It's mid-November but the weather tells otherwise. It's humid, close. The day needs a hammering thunder and rain brought to it.

The ascent is quite steep, and in deep grass. The fog doesn't lift but rather slouches away over the slope of the Down. The sky is a sheet of singular grey. I want to breathe and breathe.

We top out, me first, then Amy. Dad, overdressed, huffs.

Mum follows, cursing, wiping back her hair which has smothered itself across her face.

I simply want to get to the top.

Looking down, field after field stretches away to a flat horizon. Trees here and there, a road. A village, farms. South of us is the New Forest. I think I can see Hope Cottage, our home, winking from the edge of dim heathland and pale wood. To the north and west lies Dorset.

Amy and I hold hands and run down the face of the hill. Dew flicks up and feels like rain, a scattered mist. Our faces are cooled by the streaming air. We laugh. I hold her hand even after we have stopped, waiting by the gate for Mum and Dad. Looking back up the hill, the downward course of dew-free grass where we ran is clearly visible as two dark lines with a silvery white space between. Tracks. Our tracks. Us. Will and Amy.

Mum and Dad are going to be a while. Amy says she needs to sit down, she feels so tired. The sky lowers and a drizzle begins.

At home after lunch, Dad falls asleep by the fire in the living room.

Trying to solve the puzzle of why she feels so fatigued – and because we have been trying for a family for a while – Amy takes a pregnancy test. The result is inconclusive. She tries again. We wait, huddled in the spare room while Mum watches television and Dad snores.

A little, black positive sign appears on the screen, at first faintly, then growing solid. There is a moment of silence in which, both holding the test, we are dumbstruck. Nerves flurry, from foot to head. We look at one another and smile. I feel light, weightless. I am a father.

I cannot wait to be a dad. We hold the pregnancy test in our hands.

Our promise to one another, to keep the new pregnancy to ourselves until the first three months have passed, is immediately broken by our excitement and the need to share the good news. I tell Mum who cries, knowing how long we have been trying to conceive, and the difficulties we have gone through. She embraces us. Dad wakes with a start, his eyes bloodshot, his face full of sleep. Seeing Mum cry, he jumps up, thinking something bad has happened.

He then holds us, in a way characteristic to him, one heavy arm across my shoulders.

It's a Sunday, 20 November, 2016.

I

Hope Cottage

There are such things as swallows, Elowen.
It is hard to believe.

Shaded on the throat with the petal of an ochre rose,
long inky wings flickering,
a tail that snips and clips the air
into tangled streamers of brightness,

crafting nests that hang from fortunate homes,
looping seasons into song
through trembling hoops of return.

Placing, now, my palm upon your mother's belly
your kick takes me back
to the year's first swallow –

a sudden entrance from unimaginable distance,
a consequent lighting up of the world.

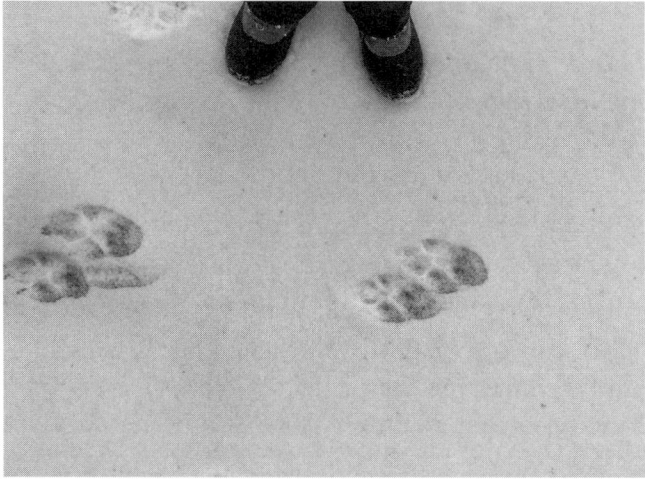

Before I even have the chance to raise my binoculars, the white-tipped eagle is long gone in the far grey, its huge serrated wings visible as a dark movement in the distant sky. Snow, released from the high fir bough that's still bouncing from the bird's departed weight, wafts and rasps into the branches below. A wind harries through the forest. The air becomes a sudden pressing of scabrous ice against my cheek. I look for the eagle between the spaces of moving trees.

A line of wolf tracks run out over the frozen, snow-covered lake. I can see, from the bank, that they form a sharp arc that swings out from the shore and back into the lake's centre where a single large boulder draws my eye. But I cannot not see where the tracks continue on from this dark rock. One by one, we cautiously step onto the ice. The wind returns, picking up the snow and spinning it out widely and thinly until it blends with the air, adding to it a cold, granular texture. The slow crunch of our boots. The stillness as we stop beside the tracks and gaze into them. The silence as we fall, each one of us mesmerised. All these things, brought together, become hypnotic.

After slowly removing the glove from my right hand, I place my bare hand lightly onto the paw marks, resting my fingers on the furthest tips of the toe, exploring its inner lines and outlines. I carefully follow its contours as though I am a child again, tracing my best friend's hand with a ball-point pen on a white sheet of paper. The snow, displaced by the moving weight of the wolf, feels different to the surrounding, untouched snow. Snow-stamped animal presence. A mood, an atmosphere, remains where they have been. My mind wanders with an imagined lone wolf, out here, loping through the snow, stopping, just as we are, to take in her surroundings. Bristling fur, her taut paws, her open eyes. The magnetism of her identity, inseparable from the landscape in which she roams.

Our guide doesn't let us go out to the boulder as it's surrounded by thin ice, a white blue ring of slush circling the dark pupil of the stone. The green trees bordering the lake are like eyelashes. I keep looking back at the boulder. I have the distinct sense that the rock – not inert but living – is watching us.

We make our way around the edge of the lake, eyes to the ground, then to the distance. We move and scan, move and scan. We listen out for a murmuring howl, or the echo of one. Two ravens peel away from the trees, lobbing out such guttural croaks that we can't help but stop. *Korp*, the guide says. *Korp*. We find no more tracks.

In the evening, as I lie in my warm bed at the guest house, the wolf is never far from my mind. I imagine the sound of her paw as it cracks the snow crust then lifts free, as she moves towards whatever drives her onward. The silence and darkness of the landscape at night, punctuated by her breathing and flood-lit by a gibbous moon, hums at my ear. My mind folds in a blanket of lunar ice. I want to be out at the lake, waiting for wolves.

I arrived the day before filled with excitement for tracking wolves, and because Amy and I have reached the fourth month of pregnancy. I feel irresponsible for leaving, though, especially as Amy has been enduring weeks of morning sickness. I have also left her to deal, single-handed, with the workload at our hostel in Snowdonia. Amy, seeing that I was torn between staying with her and following my life-long dream of tracking wolves, encouraged, even urged me to go. For the twelve years of our relationship, I have shared this obsession with her, the stories of survival and peril across the world that form a continuing thread of interest through my life.

We have been together since we were teenagers, and Amy understands, perhaps more than I do myself, how I need, at times, to be out of doors, often alone, with as little distractions as possible. I think that we understand each other enough to know, without discomfort, what each of us needs from this life. The wolves and the landscape which they are in, brings me an awakening. Eyes open, senses rapt, sharing time with these animals and the places where they live out their lives beyond mine, brings me a feeling of wholeness. The same kind of wholeness I feel when I'm with Amy, both of us standing in the midst of a love that is so much greater than our individual selves.

I think of the first time that Amy and I truly met, on the beach at night, when she pulled me down into the sea, under the waves, and the full moon was bright. We rose back up, drenched, cold, gasping. From that instant of being *grabbed* by her all those years ago, to moving to North Wales in our early twenties, when we started to renovate a dilapidated hostel to stake out a living in the mountains, our deep bond thrives when we are stretched across the edge of things. I think Amy is the main reason why I care so much about life, and about wild things left to be themselves. Just as she pulled me into the cold water all those years ago, when I could barely grow a beard and acne dotted my skin, Amy brings me close to the heart of it all.

I found it hard to switch off my phone as the plane lifted from the ground above Stansted Airport and roared up into cloud. We had suffered a missed-miscarriage the previous year, and I was convinced that I would switch on my phone when we landed in Sweden to be met with bad news. Even at nine weeks the loss of life had erased all certainty in a pregnancy. We had very little confidence. Hope was knocked off a cliff when we read the sonographer's lips: there was never even a heartbeat. A life, the beginning of our family, deposited as a dark, viscous parcel of blood and tissue in the downstairs loo at home. I held Amy so tightly. Our arms were linked for weeks afterwards.

As the plane left the runway, we had exchanged our last text messages. I closed my eyes, tried to sleep. I thought of wolves in the snow, and of the little body of life growing in Amy, a life I was already deeply in love with. After landing, I took the long journey north through Bergslagen. Evergreen tree after evergreen tree coated with snow flashed past the broad windows of the train – if I pushed my cheek against the cold glass, I could watch the carriages bending and swerving to the shape of the tracks, dark steel lines reeling beneath us.

It was dark when I arrived at the guest house in Dalarna County. Outside the red barn, two collies stared at me from cages. Sheep shuffled in a corrugated pen. Something leapt from a tree. I knocked on the blue door. There were a handful of other people at the guest house. I had originally wanted to go wolf-searching alone, but heeding Amy's insistence (after all I was going to be a dad), and the fact that I didn't actually know *where* to look for wolves, I joined an organised tour. Otherwise, I would have spent days floundering through the wilderness alone.

That night, we assembled in a bare upstairs room, with one tan leather sofa, a few Windsor-style chairs and a bay window looking out over a frozen lake, its shoreline illuminated here and there by the soft glow of cabin lights. We introduced ourselves, one by one, and explained why we were there. *Wolves*, obviously, was the main answer, followed by spending time in the winter forest, the silence. The guide gave a brief presentation on the important role the wolf plays in the health of the local ecosystem, their relationship with the moose, the way they hunt, the way they are hunted and persecuted by men, their sense of family, their wildness, how the landscape is charged with their presence. *Family* stood out for me. The close, dynamic relationships wolves uphold within their groups. In a few months, I am going to be a part of a family, a father, a dad, my group, my clan, our pack. Our guide handed round the plaster paw mark of the first wolf to return to Sweden after their extinction from the country. *Varg, Varg,* the guide says. I hold it with a keen sense of reverence.

We went looking for beavers at the edge of the lake and along the river. The water was black, the ice dark. My mind was on wolves. At first, I didn't care about the beavers. Why weren't we looking for wolves? They could be out there, near, with their families. But my impatience finally gave way to fascination as we watched the beavers diving between ice sheets, reappearing, submerging again, their eyes glistening.

The next morning I was surprised to find that I had managed to sleep straight through the night – something I rarely accomplish. The sight of a missed call from Amy on my phone made me worry that something had happened, another miscarriage, a fall. But she had only called to say good luck, and that her nausea was subsiding.

Weak light, watery orange, seeping into the dawn sky. The ice on the lake gleamed ever so slightly orange, too, a colour almost lost to itself. All the others in the group were still asleep so I decided to head out. No lights were on in the guest house. I made my way towards the lake in deep snow, raising my knees high, falling here and there between rocks and roots. I looked out across the ice, feeling content that I was in Sweden. A red squirrel darted over the snow and scratched its way along the bending bough of an aspen tree, flushing a blue tit up into the icy air. Wolf tracks, neatly littered across the lake around the boulder, brought me to my senses, into vigilance. It's all about being awake.

I didn't want to leave the lake, the tracks. The moment I turned away would be the moment a wolf would appear. The moment I wasn't thinking of Amy and our baby, something bad would happen. I had a sense that the more vigilant I could be, in my awareness of the wolves, the more keyed into their traces, the more tuned into Amy and our baby I would become.

After the others have gone to bed, the guide agrees to drive me and one other from the group back out there. It's almost midnight. We drive past the tree where we had seen the eagle. We stop at the start of an old forestry road. There are fresh tracks, and untidy splashes and streaks of urine across the verge, stark yellow in the light of the torch. And scat, dark, torn. I lean down to inspect. The tracks of one wolf lead off into the forest, on the far side of the lake where earlier in the day we hadn't had a chance to explore. In the deep forest, head-torches scanning the ground and the forest ahead, the tracks become harder and harder to pick out. The chaotic sequence of paws lunging in deep, the belly of the wolf printed into the snow, and so many other tracks of deer, perhaps moose, capercaillie, fox – scrapes, lunges, darts, glides – are hard to decipher. The forest grows more dense, interwoven, the branches clinging across one another, until we break out into a clearing that leads up to a small hill of recent logging. Hundreds of stumps bear their abrupt endings to a starry sky. A wind arrives, the trees beyond the clearing sway and seethe. By now the tracks are gone, but we carry on to the top of the hill. Out of nowhere and with no warning, the guide howls out to the night. Three howls over a few minutes. My heart races with expectancy for the wolves' reply. But only the wind answers, in brief piercing pulses of freezing air. I close my eyes tightly with the hope that the harder I close them the more acute my hearing will become. Wind running against my ear, snow falling. One silent wolf, somewhere, beneath the stars.

The next day I wake early again, early enough to see the last spill of golden dawn before the sky changes into a frozen pallet of bruised greys. We leave soon after breakfast, driving further west into another wolf's territory (each territory is roughly fifty square miles). An old road brings us to older forests untouched, as yet, by logging. The firs are thick and dangling, heavy with twirled and braided lichens, flaps of grey fungi tasselling cracked and fissured bark. In a clearing at the base of a wooded slope we find the carcass of a moose strewn open and torn. Mingled, ripped bags of flesh and bone and hairy brown skin. Blood and bare flesh, crimson lines and dots, against the pure white of the snow. The smell, as we near the carcass, makes me turn away. A wolf kill. Three wolves, perhaps, as evidenced from the direction and pattern of the tracks. As evidenced, also, from the scene, the moose was brought down further from where it was eaten into. Why was the moose moved? The scene is full of commotion in my mind, a riot of predator and prey. The running of the wolves, the chase, the moose struggling to remain upright as the wolves cling to its haunches or head, the final exasperated fall, deep snow whumphing into the air like floury, mica-peppered smoke – the actions of total surrender. Flesh still remains on the legs, the back. Layers intact or hanging loosely. What reeks most is the stomach, split open, its contents frozen.

Leaving the moose behind, we make our way further into the forest, following the direction of the wolf tracks from where they had come, where they had first seen, scented, their prey. Nearby, we stop for lunch. The lumps of resin I had picked from the pines serve as effective fuel for our afternoon fire. Despite doubling up on socks, my feet are cold in my good boots. I sit as close as possible to the flames. My boots steam. We all drink soup from kuksa cups and eat discs of rye bread. Talk comes and goes between the snapping of the fire and the silence of the landscape. A silence that is like that of someone listening, or about to speak.

I try to send Amy some photos of the day but there is no signal as I hold my phone up to the sky, aiming for unseen satellites – not that she would want gory photos of the moose carcass anyway. Scrolling through close-ups of the moose, wolf tracks, the lake, my thumb automatically stops at photos of our latest scan. Our baby's head, feet, hands. I want to show the others in the group but realising I hardly know them (I can't even remember their names) I put my phone away.

Why would any of these people care to see scan photos of my baby?

I warm my hands over the fire, throwing more pellets of pine resin into the flames. I wonder if Amy is OK at home. I think of Daisy and Dilly too, our two Welsh collies, and imagine what they would make of this landscape, their nostrils flaring at the strange and daunting air, thick with the unfamiliar smells of their ancestors.

The hour or so drive back to the guest house goes by in talk of the wolves, the moose. I can hear them running in my mind, the percussive change of tone from their paws moving from snow to ice, and back again. I register the bite of their jaw into the moose in my own jaw, my jaw bone tingling with mimicry.

Why can't we muster the courage to accommodate more wolves in the world? Why are people everything, why do we regard ourselves as the be-all and end-all? Why are we incapable of sharing this world with the wild? Will my child grow up in a world made poorer by the absence of wild wolves? I think about what it means to be a human, to be able to possess the widest possible outlook on life. Later, the questions turn and turn as I lie in bed, the red duvet half draped across my legs, flitting between my notebook, staring into the space of the small warm room, and messaging photos of my day to Amy.

After dinner, a few of us go out with the guide to a small, nameless lake west of the guest house. The moon, a round lace of white, rises above the trees surrounding the lake. The land suddenly glows as though a light is switched on from within itself. An island of trees in the middle of the frozen lake is the summer home of ospreys. The guide points out the large nest in a pine tree, flattened at the top. The ice is thick enough to walk on. The water, or pockets of trapped air, run and grumble away from our step. There is no wind. The bright moon has extinguished the stars. We meet tracks, wolf tracks. While all is luminous, crisp silver-white, the tracks are dark droplets of shadow, like black ink flicked across a blank page. The light does not reach into them. I shine a torch, and where the snow has been removed by the wolf's tread, slick ice reflects the light. Curbing the urge to follow the tracks until the early hours is as difficult as curbing the midnight cold building in my toes and fingertips. I want to follow the tracks until I find the wolf sleeping in its den, stay close to it, hidden. The night landscape gets into me. I want to blend into it as we circumnavigate the lake by the light of the moon.

The next day we leave the guest house and head two hundred miles north, driving on narrow ice-rimed roads beyond wolf territory, into government-protected land of reindeer and their Sami herders, where the wolf is heavily persecuted and very unwelcome. I still have three days left of the trip. But already I want to go home to hold Amy. I want to press my belly against hers in the shower. I want to lay my head down on her bump, to listen in on our child.

I rest my head back against the car seat and close my eyes.

*

Back in Snowdonia, I am still reeling with all that I have felt and seen. I am happy, though, to be with Amy and our baby.

We have trained up Cristen as a new staff member, to give us

22

some time off before the baby arrives – cleaning bathrooms, making beds. A couple of days later, missing the open spaces of Bergslagen, I take to the hills, sometimes with Amy, though she strains to catch her breath. Alone, going over the same old places, walking over them like my own bones, I say the name of the ridges as I scramble up them and breathe in the high air, then touch the cold waters of streams that are the arteries of the same body that is so much vaster, stronger, older than mine. On the exposed plateau north-west of the hostel, the wind has been unrelentingly cold and fierce. Deep snows have set in, blizzards scouring the tops, ridges packed out and risen to blades of whirling white, and overhung with slabs and cornices, whole rocks slick and rimed with shells of ice. I feel something like love when I pause and look around at the tall cliffs rising into the freezing mist, and below the tumbling of white waters. Across my sight, the black of a raven, the wind in its feathers, calling, calling, until she flies into the higher mists where the wind is whipping into a storm. This place still makes me feel alive, just as it did when I first moved here years ago and said, out loud, *I have to be here.*

After more long days fixing broken taps, rodding the drains clear of crammed tissues, checking-in guests, dealing with drunks, helping couples and groups plan their day hiking in the hills, I go back into the annexe with Amy. We sit together on the sofa with Daisy and Dilly, both dogs listening to the sharp wind rattling the gutters. I lie down on Amy and close my eyes, trying to listen in on our baby, trying to register the faintest twirls, kicks, movements. It calms me, just as the wind does. And before bed, around midnight, I make one last round of the hostel, empty the bins, encouraging any rowdy stragglers to get to bed. Then I step out into the garden and watch enormous clouds tower over the mountain, all lit with moonlight, like great ships taking part in some ghostly armada. Smaller clouds tear away from the towers and whip across the moon, telling of fast winds on the midnight summits.

In the day, between work shifts, I walk the easier paths with Amy, play with the dogs by the Afon Llugwy, walk the banks of the Afon

Glaslyn down into Nant Gwynant. Mostly I run, craving as much distance and height as possible.

Early spring comes on, though winter is slow to leave. The valleys are clear of snow, but in the higher passes the ice still clings. Some days, the sun is warm and bright, and then is gone in winds and rain. Winter and spring are caught in a dance. These fraught exchanges between winter and spring inject the mountains with unusual loftiness, and Moel Siabod rises above the valley where our hostel sits with an overwhelming sense of command. Below, the rivers are loud and quick. The ravens busy. The clinking of a gate latch on a nearby farm is as crisp and clear as the single strike of a bell.

The hostel is busier than ever. We feel the strain, and hope that things will calm down before the baby comes. We make the decision to run the hostel remotely from our home in the New Forest, relying more on the staff, giving them more responsibility so we can be nearer family. From the initial massive refurbishment to the day-to-day running and its round-the-clock demands, the hostel has exerted pressure on our young relationship over the years. As we neighbour the very mountainside where Thomas Firbank had his farm, on which he based his memoir *I Bought a Mountain,* we often joke that we should chronicle our own journey, titled *I Bought a Hostel.*

Leaving a busy cafe, carrying ice-creams, we make a snap decision to take a trip to Greece: a break from the hostel for Amy, and a quick, last trip before our baby is born. We feel daring, emboldened, and refuse to let our parents' concerns over the risk of flying get in the way, nor our own worries at having to leave the hostel to be run with new staff. We want to go to Kefalonia, not only for the sun after the long mountain winter, and for a break, but also to take our child to the place we honeymooned two and a half years earlier.

From the end of Beaumaris Pier, I look to the mountains. They are gone in a gloom of low cloud and rain now, save for the lower hills of the Carneddau that extend down towards the sea. The valley that runs from the coast into the Glyderau mountain range is dark with the weary colours of thick mountain rain – ashen, grey as the wet granite itself – that is being blown our way towards Anglesey. The little sunlight that we have sought by escaping the mountains for the day recedes further away towards Holyhead, until it is chased down and consumed by big rain clouds pushed along by the cold, strong wind. Snows must be deepening upon the plateaus. The strength of winter makes the beginnings of spring all the remarkable, and precious.

The wind skitters and fans across the Menai Strait. A cormorant is beaten up overhead. Then the rain hits us. Clutching our ice creams we take shelter in a wooden lean-to on the pier, close to one another, and peer out through the misting Perspex windows. There's a lone man seated on a bench behind us in another section of the shelter. He soon leaves when I start to talk like Yoda, with a lump in my throat, embarrassing Amy who hides her face in my side. I then pretend to fart. Always the clown. We laugh.

I give my unfinished ice-cream cone to Daisy and Dilly before we walk along the pier, hunkered down, faces in hoods, out of the wind and rain. Before we head back to the mountains and to the hostel, we drive out to Penmon Point. Amy stays in the car which is buffeted from side to side by the wind, while I run out along the slick and seaweed-concealed path. I am within an arm's length of the lighthouse when it suddenly becomes unreachable thanks to a swell that rises up around the base of it, sucking back down, pulling at my feet.

When I reach the car, Amy has her head down towards her belly. She is stroking her bump with both hands, making circles.

★

A girl, it's a girl, says the sonographer after spending almost thirty minutes trying to cajole our baby into the right positions, getting Amy to lie in various positions, pressing and massaging her belly. *A girl*, she says, for the third time.

I stare at the screen. *A girl*, I say, with a kind of relief. *A girl.*

I can't wait to hold her. I have always wanted a daughter, I think.

To sit with her beneath our oak tree back in the New Forest, or by a stream in the valley of Nant Gwynant, listening together, her soft voice asking, *Daddy?* To be there for her, be the best Dad I can, to make her my world – which she has already become.

On the screen, our little girl is lying down with her right leg high up, in a curious stretch. And as with all of her scans so far, she has her face half-turned away, and what expression I do see is sweetly cantankerous. At twenty weeks, our daughter is 6 inches long, or thereabout, and weighs 10 ounces. Her brain is growing rapidly. Cartilage is changing to bone, the skeleton hardening, bone marrow making blood cells. Her eyebrows are forming, giving expression to her face. She is able to swallow now, and her limbs are in proportion. Her uterus and ovaries are formed, the eggs developing. The sonographer says Amy will start, hopefully, to feel her movements soon. Quickenings.

In the car, on the way back to the hostel, driving through the mountains, the sun comes out over the Glyderau mountain range. Quartz, threading the rocks, shines. The rivers brighten, clouds clear. The land glows.

What shall we call her? Amy asks.

I take a sharp bend and drive the straight road that cuts down the Ogwen Valley. Moel Siabod looms before us.

I really like Elowen, she says. *I know we've been talking about other names, but seeing her today…I don't know… she just really suits Elowen.*

Me too, it's perfect.

It means Elm Tree in Cornish, Amy says.

It's so beautiful. I love it. Our little Elowen.

Elowen, we say together. *Elowen.*

I say the name over and over again, addicted to its rhythm. I say it with the same kind of disbelief I feel as I watch this first proper day of spring unfold in the mountains. Real warmth.

We tell family, friends. They take a few tries to say *Elowen* right.

Elowen. What a name. And the world of feeling that is in that name, and which it overspills. I write her name on any piece of paper I come across. I find myself saying it to her, my lips touching Amy's taut skin across her belly. I say her name out loud to the rivers and hills, or under my breath as I make another bed, clean another dish, vacuum another hallway, and pause, as I take the last bins down to the roadside, to say her name while looking up at the mountains. Her name, already, gives purpose to my every thought, gives shape to my every breath. She is becoming my life.

Before we head back to the New Forest, to our home, Hope Cottage, and then shortly after that, on our first family holiday to Kefalonia with Elowen, we enjoy the arrival of spring. Our last walks before leaving the hostel take us to Nant Gwynant, to the trees and the rivers. We seek out a clump of tall pine trees – four pine trees – that look out over the whole of the Nant Gwynant valley from their rocky perch upon the southern side of Y Lliwedd.

I worry about Amy making the ascent over rock and through deep heather, worry about her falling, but there is no stopping her. She always wants to see what's around the next corner, over the next hill.

Up in the pines, there's a light wind coming from the south. The pine needles tremor and whisper. Down below, the blue pools of Afon Cwm Llan are like jewels studded within the mountainside.

We christen this place, *Elowen's Pines*, and sit here for a while. *Elowen's Pines*, we say, together, holding hands, sat on the rough heather, eyes open to the mountains.

But work duties beckon. We break off our reverie and descend the quickest way, which brings us to a high stone wall. There's a gap which Amy – with a 24-week bump – just about squeezes through. At one point, she thinks she's stuck entirely, but is laughing too much to lend it any seriousness. I take a photo of her, legs out, her body under the wall.

Our final walk before heading to Hope Cottage is in Nantmor. The slim path gains height quickly to the edge of a fir wood. Amy stays here, while I go in search of a small lake I have always been intrigued by on the map but have never had the chance to find. The sun is strong. Winter is a memory now. I am gone almost an hour, and finally decide to put off finding the lake because I am concerned about leaving Amy on her own. In my haste, hopping from rock to rock, running in places, I lose my way and come suddenly to a cliff-edge. I stop just in time. To the west is the Irish Sea, and the Madog estuary bordered by golden sands. Further south, the Rhinogydd mountains bare their teeth to the sky. But I have very little idea where I am in relation to where I need to get to. Retracing my steps as closely as I can, I take another route. Then, I follow the dogs. They seem to know where to go, and they bring me to a very hidden path – not so much a path as an impression of feet. And then, dripping with sweat, my bare legs cut and bleeding from falls and scrapes, I see the fir wood, the wall. I slow down. And as I walk, I hear a voice. A singing voice. It's Amy, singing Elowen's song. Brahms' Lullaby. *Baby Els, Baby Els, Baby E-LO-W-E-N...*

She is so lost in her own happy world of mother and daughter she hasn't even noticed I've been gone for more than an hour. I stay back a little while, hidden from view, and listen to Amy's sweet voice in the wild surroundings.

I am relieved to have found them.

*

One swallow, two, three, then more than twenty burst into view from behind the trees, scattering in a clipping throng, skimming low, and lower again, over the blue water – the lightest of blues – of Kimilia cove. Ripples run to the waveless water's edge as they snip the surface for flies, and lift, wheel back, take to the air, and swoop down again. Their reflections on the water shrink as they fast approach them, disappear, then reappear again when the swallows ascend and fly away, leaving their reflections to chase them.

Sitting up from laying my head on the warm skin of Amy's belly, listening to Elowen, talking to her, saying her name, feeling her movements, her kicks and thumps and body-rolls against my cheek, I want to go swim beneath the shower of swallows.

Amy scoots back into the cliff-shadow, out of the midday sun. With our rucksack as her pillow, she lies down and closes her eyes. Only her feet are in the sun. The walk here was hot and tiring but Amy being Amy didn't want to turn back. The narrow footpath, leading from our hotel, through dense woods of sun-gnarled oak and cypress, the aroma of Mediterranean flowers, rosemary, bay, thyme, the woods loud with bees and insects, affording teasing glimpses of the turquoise waters – and turquoise being Amy's favourite colour – was too irresistible.

As I walk down to the water's edge, using the smooth, white pebbles as stepping-stones, I keep looking back at Amy. Because her head is tilted down lower than her pregnant tummy, from where I stand she is all belly and legs, beautiful, round, and pale like the pebbles that surround her. Her dark hair is fallen about her shoulders.

The cold touch of the water upon my toes shakes me out of my reverie. As it's only early May, the water isn't warm. Only a few swallows are now darting over the water, flitting as light and as soundless as moths. As I am closer to them, I can see the vivid red patches of their throats that throttle and vibrate as they break out into chattering song when I disturb the stillness of the water, enter the sea, and swim into the arena of their flying. They soon vanish into the sky behind the dark curtain of cliffside trees, heading, by the diminishing sounds of them, towards Ithaca.

Closing my eyes and floating on my back, I feel the weariness of the past weeks and months. The demands of the hostel have not relented since we first got the keys; even yesterday, as we boarded the plane, Amy got a message from Cristen to say that she'd already had enough, and was quitting without notice, leaving the hostel, that sleeps sixty in total, abandoned to a week's worth of pre-booked guests.

In this blue space of peace, I think of all the swallows that Elowen will see. It's a little dream of mine – one of a series of a father's wishes, such as when I lift her up to touch the face of the full moon – to see what her reactions will be when she sees them flying outside her window at home in the New Forest, settling on the sagging wire that runs from our roof to the neighbour's house, the sight of them hunting out on the heath, and the swallows that have nested beneath the hostel fire escape for years, enduring the harsh weathers of Snowdonia.

As the water buoys me up beyond all worry into the sun, and a sense of deep fulfilment I have not known before takes hold of my weight, I am suddenly woken by a splash. It is Amy. She is swimming towards me. I swim towards her, and we hold one another. Her legs are wrapped around me. Her eyes sparkle in the sun, emerald and hazel jewels. Her freckles have bloomed. We touch foreheads, kiss, and tread water together.

I dive down and hold Amy's tummy, kiss her belly button in the clear, blue water. I shout *Elowen, Elowen!* under water, the bubbles of my breath rising up. Then we swim together, exploring the edges of the cove, the inlets and caves and places where the trees overhang the water, all the way to where the cove opens out to the rougher, deeper, darker waters of the Straits of Ithaca swept by winds and painted with dancing lights.

Two and a half years ago Amy and I spent our Honeymoon in this very same hotel, located on a low cliff-edge at the forested, northern tip of Kefalonia, with views out towards Ithaca, and views, slightly further round to the most southern tip of Lefkada. We spent a week on each of these three islands. And as I look out towards Ithaca, holding a railing that runs along the edge of a low cliff which tapers down to a small, rocky inlet where kayaks are docked and the choppy sea heaves and falls around a floating pontoon, I think of that trip, taken only days after our wedding in the garden at Hope Cottage. On Ithaca, we walked hand in hand along quiet streets, and returned every day to an almost inaccessible cove, found at the end of a pine forest where tree roots erupted onto the stones, and green needles floated on the water. On Lefkada, we sought out the quiet places, just as we always have – the places where we feel there is only us in the world. I recall that even when we first started dating, back in our teens, we both used to say we wished we were animals. We said it with such intensity and belief as though it could be a real possibility to not be human anymore. A kind of magic, our own magic.

Leaving Amy to sleep the afternoon away by the pool, I take a kayak out to the far tip of a narrow isthmus of white, serrated rock, that juts out into the Straits of Ithaca. The warm wind blows hard, knocking the kayak against the rocks which shelve off into darkness. On our honeymoon, my wedding ring fell from my finger in the cove just round from here. Two Dutch divers, taking a rest on the beach, found it. I was speechless. On the way back I crossed my middle-finger over my ring-finger in a clasp to keep the ring safely on. Jellyfish bobbed by. The wind pushed me back. I was gone hours, and on my return I was met by Amy who stood waiting for me, full of worry, on the dock.

This time, I will not leave her and Elowen for long, so instead of taking the kayak further along the coast, I paddle to the base of the Isthmus, and slide and scrape onto a small beach of white stones. Lobbing the paddle and dragging the kayak up, I lie down on the warm, wet stones. My skin tingles in the sun. The wind runs over me.

Every day I do this, sometimes swimming the few kilometres from the hotel to this beach, or taking the kayak. After each small journey I come back to Amy who is either sleeping or reading or has her hands interlaced like tender boughs over her tummy. As I walk up from the pontoon I see Amy's lips moving. Private whispers, private songs and conversations with Elowen. I sit down, still dripping from my long swim, and join my hand and hers. At twenty-eight weeks now, Elowen can sense, see, light filtering in through the womb. She must be blinking, her eyelashes flickering in the womb-light. Kefalonia light. The same light that has me squinting, that has burnt my shoulders, and which has browned her Mum's hands and brought out her constellations of freckles.

Elowen's heart rate is about 140 beats per minute now. I try to listen in on her, tucking my ear in as close as possible. I think I can, but I am not sure. Soon I will be able to. But I can definitely feel the strong, rounded push of her head into my palm, and the glide of her foot which, given, time, will run. Our hands wait in tense anticipation for the next kick as though it's some kind of game.

*

June is hot and bright. Swallows flit from the wire that stretches between Hope Cottage, and our neighbour's house, Little Orchard. A pair have nested in the log shed, they swing in and out all day long through the half-door which I leave open.

Back from Kefalonia, we hunker down at Hope Cottage. Amy is far too pregnant now to make the long drives north to Snowdonia for work. I miss the mountains. But it's time to prepare our home for Elowen, *to nest*, as Amy calls it, to be nearer family, to slow down and get things in place for our little girl. Elowen is like a horizon drawing closer every day, every minute, every heartbeat and breath, brightening, coming towards us as we are drawn towards her.

In the evening, nightjars drill their frank tunes into the air. The heath is loud with their weird, wobbling trill. There is no breeze, our room is stifling. When the full moon comes, I walk out onto the heath where the nightjars dwell and try to spot their moonlit eyes in the gorse. All I can think about is bringing Elowen beneath the moon, to see her face in moonlight. I'm eager now to lay my hand on her warm head, to feel her weight in my arms, for her to be near my body, too, and to hear my voice.

Up the four-mile stretch of Shell Bay, Studland, on the Dorset coast, the wind doesn't find us. In fact, there's hardly any wind at all. At thirty-six weeks pregnant, Amy has done well to get here, trudging in the heat through deep, soft sand, up and around, over and down sand dunes, and through mazes of thick marram grass that spiked our bare legs.

We have found our spot – a place I've been visiting since childhood. There's nobody else around. A distant haze shimmers above the sand.

A warm breeze comes in, a hesitation of air, too gentle and restrained to move the sand. Each grain is perfectly still. We are so used to the wind blowing a hooley off the sea here – long ropes of sand whipping this way and that, flicking into mouths and eyes, the dogs squinting and wincing. The stillness, like the stillness of being in the dunes, feels good.

The dogs paddle by the water's edge, run up, down, up and down the shore that is being revealed by the lowering of the tide. We have timed our visit just right. Soon, there will be pools dotted far and wide, some shallow, some deep, all shining in the sun.

For now, Amy and I lie close together beneath the shade of a crooked umbrella that we bought years ago on our first holiday to Greece. I feel relaxed enough to read a book. Amy too.

Now and again I look over my book, or past it, at Amy and Elowen, and beyond them at the surroundings, the backdrop of the sea and the blue, summer sky buoyant with swallows. What is that feeling, when things seem to come right, as if steered into place? I feel a sense of calm, or settlement.

We are ready, not only in the practical sense of having the house kitted out – the cot assembled, new shelving put up, nappy-changing stations, bottles, bibs, wall-murals, blankets, clothing, and more – but ready because *our* time as parents has come. All Elowen has to do is arrive into the space that is ready for her. She is here already, though, in the darkness, hearing, moving, listening, breathing, feeding, waiting, waiting until that moment comes.

Soon there will be another person with us. Another pair of hands, eyes, feet. Hair to comb, a body to wash, a tummy to feed. And, beyond that early period of time when the newborn fills the house, there will be her explorations of the wider world. Adventures in touch, taste, smell, sound. I long to see her press her feet on the wet sand at the shore's edge, and totter from the breaking waves with Amy and me at her side. I can hardly wait for the first time she will be stopped in her tracks by the sight of a gleaming shell. The world will be amazing, and I want to see that world too.

Sometimes my heart bursts with all the memories that we are going to make together. And I feel it all now. A sense of pride in my family comes over me when I look at them. From the first moment Amy took the pregnancy test and our dreams were realised, it would never just be us anymore. We are all part of one another's life.

I place my book down and plunge my hands into the soft, warm sand. Digging down with my fingers, rummaging, I find the deeper layer of coolness where the sun can't reach. My hands stall. I keep them there until I curl my fingers, gathering handfuls of cool wet sand, dredging carefully up to the surface.

*

It's three weeks until Elowen's due date, July 27th. There's a sense of momentum now, in time, and in getting things done. I work hard to finish off the fencing along our field edge – my own way of *nesting* – while Amy works hard in the house, painting the nursery walls. We assemble the cot together outside in the front garden. I take pictures of Amy with Daisy and Dilly beside her.

Having spent so much time in Snowdonia we have been unable to attend any NCT classes, but we manage to get to the final one in town. Amy is embarrassed by my Volvo as it squeaks and squeals when I turn into the car park – an old banger purchased purely for its comic effect when I pick Elowen up from school one day; I can see her cheeks blush with embarrassment. There are other couples there, most of whom have attended from the beginning. We feel like newcomers, late on the scene. The midwife goes through what to expect on the day of the birth. She gives tips to the dads on how to comfort their partners during labour. Back home, I practice the massage techniques on Amy with the same thoroughness as if preparing for a vital exam.

My mum joins Amy's Mum and sister at Elowen's thirty-eight week scan. We booked it because we were getting impatient to see her. It will really show our baby girl, and give us all the chance to share in our excitement. Again, the little tike is facing away, but after some gentle persuasion by the sonographer, she turns around and presents her face, her pudgy cheeks and sullen brow, which I just want to kiss.

She's thriving, the sonographer says. *Measuring quite large, but nothing to be concerned about at all,* she adds, pointing at the graph.

Back home, we pore over Elowen's growth during the past few months, laying down photos of each scan in order, starting with the twelve-week one, the first trimester. This was a real milestone. Her estimated delivery was given at the end of July, and it was the first time Amy and I were told that the baby was growing in the right place and appeared healthy. We were so grateful that she had come so far.

We carry on, inspecting every detail of the small photographs, amazed at her development, from no more than three inches long during the early stages to being capable of hiccups, with eyelids formed as frail as frost, her nose and ears and an upper lip, those toes curling or uncurling, hands that can hold and let go in reflex, the kick of legs and lift of arms that will one day hold me. And what about all the things we cannot see? Her nervous system, growing, expanding, changing – neural networks building and strengthening. Cells budding, muscles thickening, the layers delineating and interconnecting, oxygen riding its way through blood-vessels. The primal organs: the kidneys, the heart, the brain, the stomach. This life within Amy. I cannot help but think of Elowen's future; I cannot wait to show her our favourite oak tree. Her future, our dreams and aspirations as parents. What we imagine for her and how we imagine her to be, seem as definite as the actual growth of her body. Those heartfelt imaginings – first feed, first words, first steps, first days at school, first snow, first leaf-fall, and further on again – are all part of Elowen's picture, along with her feet, her toes, her hands, her eyes.

Studying the scan photos intensely, as if trying to commit them to memory, I hear Elowen's fast heartbeat in my ears, in my mind: the gallop I heard in the scanning room when the midwife first located the baby and projected the sound of her heartbeat into the room with the Doppler. The sound stirred me deeply, like nothing I had ever heard before. And surrounding that rapid gallop of the heart, the river-like plunge and whispering whoosh of blood flowing.

One scan photo stands out in particular: Elowen is facing us, looking, it seems, directly at us, and is upright, on feet that are hardly visible, centred within the dark window of the womb. We laugh, but are also taken aback by her confrontational stance, her bold greeting. Our sense of our child's character is already starting to build, becoming as real as the sound of her movements when I lay my ear on the soft skin of Amy's belly, and feel Elowen's kicks or thumps against my cheek when I say her name. *Elowen, Elowen.* She knows our voices. She must even know the barking of Daisy and Dilly.

We're given a tour of the birthing ward by a senior midwife at Southampton General, which also gives me the opportunity to practice, again, the route here.

With only a week to go, I spend the time carving a spoon and cup and little plate for Elowen out of alder wood from a windfall in the woods behind our house. I even re-carve the old *Hope Cottage* plaque at the front, giving it a new coat of oil, bringing out the grain in the wood, emboldening the letters and the sense of home.

We see friends, take small walks. Every morning I head out to the oak tree and weave through the branches, dreaming of bringing Elowen here so we can sit together in the wide saddle where the branches part. Further into the woods, though still with a view of the oak, I make a small fire with birch logs and sit with the flames. The wind seems to grow through the forest. The trees, particularly the pines, sound astounded, as though breathlessly asking for a rest before the next intake of air, each wave rolling out and over the heath. I will bring Elowen here as soon as she can stand. She'll share a drink from my kuksa cup. We can sit together beside a small birch fire, shifting to avoid the smoke or to glimpse one or two deer, walking undisturbed, carrying bags of secrets down to the stream. We will listen to the wind growing in the trees.

I watch all my dreams, a dad's dreams, with the same focus as I watch the flames fading on the logs. I put the fire out and bury the charred wood in earth before heading home.

★

We all get together on the Sunday at my parents' house for a family barbecue. Amy says she doesn't feel up to it − Elowen kicked wildly in the night. The summer rain doesn't relent as Amy rests in an armchair in the living room. She looks tired but happy. Children and dogs run amok in the garden. My brother's children put butterfly stickers all over Amy's belly, and shriek when they feel Elowen's sudden kicks. Dad lifts a glass to toast how happy he feels to see us all together.

Back home at 9 p.m., tired out but content, we sit together at the end of the table and each eat a bowl of Crunchy Nut.

The house, at this time of night, with the rain silencing the nightjars, is so quiet.

II

Elowen

My breath strays across the moon,
or the breath of one close by who,
when I turn,
is gone. You did not breathe outside
so it cannot be you.

Dew turns to frost where I stand.
An owl falls away into darkness.
Echoless, flapping against branches.

The following morning I wake to find Amy moving her hands over her bare tummy, stroking and pressing her skin. She is sat up, the pregnancy pillow wrapped around her. The room is bright and warm. Sitting up with her, I put my hand on her belly. She is quiet, totally absorbed in looking at her bump.

Everything OK? I say, but Amy doesn't answer. I ask again. Amy looks at me. Her eyes are withdrawn. She looks pale. *Have you been up for a while?* Again, she doesn't answer. I begin to feel the concern in her expression now that sleep has left me.

What's wrong, what's wrong? I ask.

I haven't felt Elowen this morning. I've been awake for an hour already.

Well, she's probably engaged now, getting ready to be born. That's what the midwife told us last week.

You're probably right, can you go get me a cold drink, and a bowl of cereal?

Sure, I say, getting out of bed.

Leaving the room, I look back at Amy – there's a strong look of worry in her face, and she pushes on her belly quite hard, twice.

As I get downstairs, stroking and hugging Daisy and Dilly on my way to the kitchen, there's a thud on the front door. The electrician. I had forgotten he was coming at eight to wire in the new smoke alarms and chase in new lights in Elowen's room. I'm conscious that Amy is waiting for me upstairs so I quickly unlock the door, exchange niceties, then get to the kitchen, pouring out the last of the Crunchy Nut that we'd eaten the night before, and running the tap long enough to get the coldest water. The electrician goes to say something but I rush upstairs, past the dogs, who are eager to be fed their breakfast too.

Amy's face is even paler, desperate. *She's not moving at all, nothing. You try. She always kicks when you say her name.*

While Amy gulps down the water and eats the cereal, I lean in close and say, loudly, *Elowen… Elowen… Elowen…*

We wait.

Again, *Elowen, Elowen, Elowen,* calling her name as if summoning her in from the rain.

Can you call Mum, Amy says, *and get her to come look after the dogs and see to the electrician. We should go into hospital.*

As we live in the forest, with trees all around, there's no signal on our mobile phones, so I squeeze past the electrician busy on a ladder in the hall, and call Amy's mum on the house phone. She answers immediately. My voice is shaking, my hands too.

I think Elowen is going to be born today, so we're just going to get into hospital.

Have Amy's waters broken? she asks.

No, but Amy can't feel her so she must be engaged or something…

After a pause, Amy's mum says she'll be at ours in ten minutes.

When I get back upstairs, Amy is already changed and ready to leave. I grab the pregnancy pillow, as well as our hospital bag. She holds on to her belly with both hands.

Outside, it's bright and hot. The car is packed. Elowen's car seat put in. I load the car with a few extra things, growing more sure that I'm going to meet our daughter soon. *Everything is fine, everything is fine,* a voice says to me.

When Amy's mum arrives, I give the dogs a big hug and say goodbye. I say thank you to Amy's mum with a smile, and clamber into the car. She smiles back. Watching us leave, she closes the gate.

Down the road, Amy tries again to stir Elowen. She thinks she feels something, maybe a kick, maybe a nudge, something. I put on music, a song that Elowen has come to respond to during our evenings in watching *The Vikings*, 'If I Had a Heart' by Fever Ray. Amy turns the volume high. Then holds her belly. Nothing. At the song's end, she turns the music off and bursts into tears.

On the motorway, I grip the steering wheel until my knuckles whiten, reaching 90 mph before I turn off for Southampton General. Having practiced the route so many times over the months, it's second nature to me. Soon we see hospital signs, the large H bringing relief to my nerves. I run a red light, a car sounds its horn. A voice in my head is still going, *Everything is fine, this can't be happening, everything is fine, this can't be happening.*

Amy gets out at The Princess Anne Maternity Ward, not even closing the door behind her. I watch her go through the double doors, through a group of builders laying new slabs at the entrance, past a woman who is heavily pregnant and smoking. Amy doesn't look back.

The car parks are chock-full, barriers slow to lift, people emerging from behind cars, taking to the lifts, the stairs. Far away from The Princess Anne Ward, I find what seems like the last space, which is so tight I have to scramble into the back of the car and out of the boot to get out. There's a queue at every ticket machine. I stand in line for a while, then abandon it as a sense of urgency overcomes me – the thought of Amy alone in the ward with her fears. I leave all our things in the car. I run to her.

At the reception desk, I ask for *Amy Searle.* The woman points to the waiting room. When I enter the room, there's only one seat available, across from Amy in a busy room of other expectant parents. Amy is sat between two other pregnant women, both of them talking and smiling with their partners. Amy and I look across at one another. The room goes totally silent even though other people's mouths are moving. She is so beautiful. Everything blurs except for Amy, who I see so clearly across from me, framed as in a window of our own world.

I do not know how long we have waited when a voice calls *Amy Searle?* Holding hands, we follow a midwife down a long corridor and into a room lined with beds and machines. The room is loud with galloping heartbeats, the whir and beating rush of blood-flow picked up by the Dopplers that various midwifes are pressing onto bellies.

Curtains are drawn around us. A midwife steps through, bringing the Doppler closer to the bedside. Before she speaks, Amy says, leaning up on her elbows, *I haven't felt our baby today.*

The midwife locates Elowen using her hands them squeezes gel onto Amy's tummy and begin to move the Doppler over and around her belly.

What's your baby's name? the midwife asks.

Elowen, we say together, proudly.

That's a beautiful name, the midwife replies, still moving the disc, still searching.

There's a look in the midwife's eyes I haven't seen before, as she searches and searches. This is the longest it's taken for Elowen's heartbeat to be found. I hold Amy's hand tightly, seated beside her.

I watch the midwife's every move. Time passes. Then she stops, lifting the disc from Amy's belly, and undoes the straps from around her. She stands up, then switches the machine off.

She steps through the curtains. I look at Amy who is weeping into her right hand that is clasped over her face.

I do not understand what's happening.

Another woman enters, not a midwife, a doctor. She says *Hello* and asks if we could follow her. She leads us past all the other mums and dads, through the auditorium of infant heartbeats, through a door, and into darkness and quiet. We are in a room with a single bed, a desk, and a computer.

Amy lies down. I stand. The doctor sits down behind the computer, then stands to wheel over an ultrasound machine.

All I see is darkness, the blur of the doctor's face, a faint colour of blonde in her hair, strip blinds half open across a large window that looks out towards somewhere with grass and trees. And Amy lying down on the bed as the doctor, just like the midwife before, searches for a heartbeat.

She stops, lifts the disc away, wipes away the gel from Amy's skin with a tissue. She leans over and switches the off the screen. Charts and images and numbers go dark and blank. She sits back down at the desk.

There's a pause.

I'm sorry, but your baby has died.

The words go through me with the sharpness of a blade. The floor is taken away from under me.

The room is dark, like nightfall. I turn to Amy who has her head buried in her hands. The doctor stands, slowly. A scream. I hear Amy's mum's voice, though it sounds faint, so far away. Outside in a hospital garden, I can hardly breathe. Mum is with me, like a shadow.

They are wrong, they are wrong, it's all a mistake, it's all a mistake, this is what I hear myself say.

Dad has come too, though I can't see his face. I feel his embrace. I hear anger. I am in a corridor. It is bright and white. My back slides down the cold wall and I am on the floor. Faces over me. Faces burying me.

Amy, where is Amy? I want Amy.

I find her, I see her, I touch her, I hold her. She is shaking.

A midwife enters the room. A heavy folder is passed to me. Leaflets, pamphlets, booklets, purple and crimson butterflies. (An image arrives in me, of my brother's children placing butterflies on Amy's belly yesterday afternoon.) *Caring for the Bereaved. Losing a Child.* A hand takes it from me that I half-recognise. I hear Amy's voice, and go towards it. She is not as far away as I thought.

Amy has questions. *How will she come out? Do I have to give birth to her? Can I have a caesarean to get her out today?* The midwife is talking to her, explaining what will happen next. There's an overwhelming mood of gathering momentum, but I'm not sure what that is.

You will be induced. We'll give you pills today that will move things along, stimulate those hormones. That will get the baby ready to come out. Go home, try and get rest. Come back 8am on Wednesday. You have a bit of time to go home and be with your family, your baby.

I can see us leaving. We walk back through the bright and busy room, loud with heartbeats.

I'm sorry but your baby has died.

I hear those words again and see the face that said them.

Outside it is bright. The car is there, where I left it.

I see myself driving home. I see Amy and I outside Hope Cottage in the sun. Amy's dad is waiting for us there, crying into Amy's shoulder. *It's OK, Dad, it's OK,* Amy says, stroking the back of his head.

There's a sheet or towel over every mirror in the house. Family are in the house, footsteps and echoes, though I cannot hear or see them as a whole people, only snapshots of colour, fragments of sound in an ache of darkness.

We sing Elowen's song to her in the shower. *Baby Els, Baby Els,* but we cannot finish it. *She's alive, she can hear me. They've made a mistake.*

We hold one another on the bed, and swear to love one another no matter what, and that everything will be OK because we have one another. We lie on our sides on the bed for most of the day, holding one another's faces, nose pressed to nose.

Do we walk the dogs in the woods and out across the heath? Do we keep holding one another, breathing the same air? Should we eat or drink? Are we asleep, or awake? Where and what are we? Am I hearing the howls of Amy, or is that cry inside me?

At night, I put my hand on Amy's belly, and feel Elowen kick, and roll, and kick again. I speak to her, my lips against skin. *I love you Elowen, I love you so much.* I quickly withdraw my hand as though I have made a transgression.

*

I'm awake before the alarm goes at 7 a.m., my eyes stinging from tears.

The white towel is still draped over the bedroom mirror, placed there on Monday after returning from the hospital. Amy cannot bear to see the reflection of her pregnant belly, now more sagged, dropped. There are earrings and necklaces hung up beside Amy's dresser, drawers half open, clothes on the floor. It's the same room, but entirely different. From the bed, I look at these familiar things as daylight glows around the borders of the drawn curtains. I can hear voices downstairs – Amy's dad, Phillip, and her mum, Jane, and sister, Hannah, and my mum, too. Muffled words in the kitchen below. The kettle boiling, the clanking of cups as they are pulled from a drawer. Amy has turned away from me, half concealed in the pregnancy pillow she bought a few weeks ago to help ease her sciatica. It has also helped to stop her rolling onto her back in the night. Before she got the pillow, I would always nudge her back onto her side, taking the advice from the midwives seriously that lying on her back could harm our baby.

I think she's still asleep until I can see her shoulders and back shaking and heaving in movements that tell me she's crying. I roll over and bury my face in her hair. My habit has always been to put my hand on her belly, to feel for Elowen's kicks, but I don't know what to do so it hovers over her tummy. Amy thinks that she can feel Elowen moving.

We sit up together. I do not want to open the curtains. We undress together and step into the bath. I hold Amy with care, in the way I have been holding her for months now, to protect Elowen. Facing one another, belly to belly, Elowen cushioned between us. I turn on the shower and watch the water flow over us and pool in the space where our bellies meet. Amy sings Elowen's song, Brahms' Lullaby, *Baby Els, Baby Els, Baby E-lo-wen …*

I spread my right hand over Amy's belly, my sense of touch so used to feeling Elowen's movements, my hand waiting there long after my mind knows that there is no response but stillness. I kneel and press my cheek against Amy's belly. I close my eyes and listen, listen, listen.

Only a few days ago there was our daughter's heartbeat. Only a few days ago I would say *Elowen* and she would kick back hearing Daddy's voice. Only a few days ago I thought today was going to be the most precious day in my life.

We dry one another after the bath. I open the window and let out the steam, the hazy warm air quickly clearing to reveal Amy's face. I look into her eyes.

Jane calls up to us, saying it's almost time to leave. I can hear the paws of Daisy and Dilly drumming on stairs as they run to see us. Daisy's mistimed gait, Dilly's cumbersome upward leap, as familiar as their yaps and barks. They push their way into the bathroom, tails wagging, ears pinned back. Kneeling down, wrapped in towels, Amy and I hold their heads into our chests.

I cannot eat any breakfast. Hannah, who stayed the night on the sofa, offers to feed the dogs but I do it, wanting the normal routine to somehow continue. Amy's Mum and sister pack the hospital bag as we cannot bear to do it again, keeping Amy's pillow separate as it's too big to fit.

A surge of hope comes through now and again as I load the car, the hospital has got it all wrong, Elowen's heart will suddenly beat back to life. Even now, I cannot shake off the hope that Elowen will be delivered, safe and warm. It has all been a big misunderstanding.

I remove the baby seat that I had painstakingly installed and fussed over for hours a few days ago, going over and over the instructions to ensure a proper fit. I hardly notice the weather, the colour of the sky or the trees. I pay little attention to the New Forest ponies gathered at the gate, rubbing their necks on the pointed pails of the fence, or drinking from puddles that haven't dried out, it seems, since winter. I take a deep breath, the air shaking down my throat into my lungs that feel tight, restricted. It is summer now, but I feel cold and weak.

We leave the dogs behind. Dilly jumps up onto the windowsill, looking at us as we get into the car. They will stay at Jane's again, looked after by Amy's stepdad. I sit in the back with Amy, holding her hand, as Philip drives us to the hospital. We say very few words, except *I love you* as we turn off the motorway and follow the H signs to the hospital, taking the same route I had practiced.

It's exactly 8 a.m. when we arrive at the hospital. We make our way through the swinging doors of the Princess Anne Maternity Ward, carrying the turquoise suitcase, with the pregnancy pillow wrapped around and draped over my shoulders. When passing people – nurses, doctors, families, one family following their daughter holding her newborn baby on her chest, her eyes half-closed in deep contentment, as she is wheeled on a bed across us and in full view, straight on through doors that shut on us as we approach them. I wonder if they see that Amy is pregnant and assume that this is a special day for us. One mother, standing beside a vending machine, hands pressed into her lower back, her belly bulging and rubbed by her husband, gives us a celebratory smile in the midst of her deep and concentrated breathing. The pursed O-shape of her mouth falls into the line of a smile as we pass her.

Amy stands behind me as we give our names at reception. They are expecting us. A midwife comes out to greet us and takes us down the long ward towards our room. It's Nina, the same midwife who consoled us after we found out that Elowen had died, and she walks us to the room in which Elowen will now be delivered. We are escorted away from the main birthing area, past the birthing pools that we had originally planned to use, and down a long, empty corridor. It's quiet. A broken wall light flickers. Our room is around another corner, set away from the other delivery rooms. The corridors are empty, footsteps echo far off, moving away from us. There are no lights on in the adjacent rooms. Voices mumble behind doors that read *Staff Only*.

Nina is positive. She's young, her face radiant and incongruous against the dour and clinical surroundings. Phillip and Jane arrive. As does Hannah, who drove here separately. I haul the bags. Amy sits at the foot of the bed, holding her tummy, her Elowen.

Nina tells Amy that the hormones she took on Monday will soon take effect, kick-starting her body towards labour. For now, we simply have to wait. I message my mum to tell her we've arrived, and give her the ward and room number.

As the morning progresses, the small room starts to warm up, becomes stuffy, close. I try to slide up a window but it only opens an inch. Our room is high up and overlooks a courtyard of broken stone slabs, an old fountain, now derelict and overgrown with weeds. There's a wooden bench tipped over on its back, and a bird feeder toppled and rotten. When a breeze finally comes, finding the one-inch gap, I feel I can breathe again. I think of the stand of silver birch trees not far from our home, shimmering in the wind.

Nina is often in the room, either checking on Amy, taking her blood pressure, heart rate, asking if she can feel anything like contractions, twinges, or distracting us with anecdotes about her travels, her dating life, which keeps our minds off the reality of what's happening. Every hour or so she checks if Amy is dilated.

Amy's step-dad makes a visit. I ask how the dogs are getting on, uplifted by the idea of Daisy and Dilly running through the forest, chasing squirrels and deer through the mud. My dad comes in intermittently, as does Amy's step-mum. Family are always with us in the room, either bringing water, food, or sitting with us, talking. When I sit on the reclining chair, it collapses, making everyone laugh.

We watch television but switch it off at exactly noon when Amy starts to feel a tightening pain in her lower back. Apparently, the drugs used for an induction are much powerful when the baby is not alive. The baby cannot move, wriggle. Amy has to do everything. The pain so much more acute than a live delivery.

She breathes, heavily, slowly, rhythmically, just like we practiced together after the last NCT class. Amy arches over the bed. I massage her lower back, moving in circles and spreading my hands up either side of her spine, and down again, taking care and pride just as I rehearsed it. After a little while, Amy is in too much pain to find it of any benefit. She lies down, her pallor deteriorating. She begins to shiver. She keeps saying she's cold, freezing, her whole body quaking as she tries to walk around the bed. By now, there are no family members in the room. Jane and Hannah and my mum come in intermittently, but I barely notice them.

Nina brings in a doctor who, after assessing Amy, administers intravenous antibiotics to counteract the infection that is building up in her body – there is concern that Amy may have Sepsis Nina gives her gas and air. Amy reclines on the bed with a mask over her face, and breathes. I stare at her from my low chair beside the bed, holding her hand too tightly.

The gas and air is ineffective. Nina talks Amy through a series of rhythmic breathing exercises. I count Amy's breaths, breathing in time with her. She clutches the mask and yanks it off her face. Nina presses a large green button. A small red light appears. The gas and air was not properly turned on. She places the mask back over Amy's mouth and nose, saying *Sorry, sorry Amy.*

As the gas and air begins to ease Amy's pain and building sense of panic, and the antibiotics are winning against the infection, I see life return to Amy's face, blood blushing her cheeks, freckles appearing.

She turns to me and almost smiles. Then the smile erupts into laughter, laughter that doesn't stop. In her delirium, she tries to crack jokes, slips into her native Lancashire dialect, and then she weeps and weeps. I stand and lean over her, holding on. Her hospital gown is damp with sweat, her arms weak as she tries to put them around me.

By late afternoon, the clock on the wall has become a countdown to Elowen's birth. I could stand up at any moment and leave the room, go outside for air, and I try to. But whenever I stand in the corridor outside the room, I immediately turn back in. I cannot leave Amy.

Amy is given morphine once the contractions begin. By 8 p.m. the anaesthetist arrives to give Amy the epidural, an hour later than planned. He makes a point of saying that his shift finished half an hour ago, which I don't care about. But when Nina's shift comes to an end, we are deflated to see her leave. She reassures us that we'll be in safe hands with the next team of midwives, and that she'll be with us first thing in the morning.

Phillip and Jane and my mum are back in the room with us. The doses of morphine have brought Amy into a state of pain she can bear, a kind of balance. She is drowsy, though, and not fully aware of her surroundings. To administer the epidural, Amy has to get into the correct position. Phillip and I support her as she sits up and turns to face the window side of the room. Amy leans over, her head on my shoulder. Nina comes back, even though her shift has ended, and gently unties Amy's gown. The anaesthetist stands behind Amy, and talks her through the procedure, telling us all about the potential risks. It's imperative that she stay still and as straight as possible, leaning on me for support, even through the contractions that are pulsing through her now. Phillip is right beside us, talking to her about the importance of breathing, of staying calm. He and I breathe out and breathe in. Amy's water's break. As we count to ten with every exhalation, the needle pierces into Amy's back, pinching the skin as it slides in at the exact point along the spine where the drug is deemed most effective. A tassel hangs from the needle that is then attached to the tube through which the drug will flow. I worry that when Amy lies back down, the needle will snag in the bedding.

The room is too crowded when my family and Amy's are in it, so the midwife asks that only me and one other person are present, giving more space for her to attend to Amy.

While I am alone with Amy, the midwife broaches the pressing subject of whether or not we wish to see Elowen being born or for a screen to be put up. We ask for a screen because we don't know why she died and we are scared of what she might look like.

By midnight, twelve hours since the inducement drugs took effect, Amy is exhausted. It has also become evident that the epidural has not been effective throughout Amy's body. She does not want to feel the pain of the birth, and yet she can feel the full force of it concentrated in her left lower side where the epidural hasn't worked. The anaesthetist is called, the epidural repeated. But it seems too late now as her contractions are gaining in power and taking on a definite rhythm.

The next hour becomes an endurance of breathing and pushing, breathing, pushing. The midwife explains that because the baby is not alive, it will be much harder for her to be delivered, and that she won't be able to get into the position a living baby would get into.

I massage the area of acute pain in Amy's side with all my strength and, when it is ready, press the green button to release more morphine into her body.

A midwife who I have not seen before quietly enters the room and leaves a box on the table by the window, with *Memory Box* inscribed in italics. On it, there's a picture of a teddy bear holding a balloon, and on top of the box there's a thick white folder labelled *Caring for the Bereaved* with yet more butterflies, arranged in a swerving line from small to big. Elowen, though, is not a memory. I tell midwife to put the box and folder somewhere else, out of sight. I do not want Amy to see it. A box of trinkets, souvenirs.

Two midwives, Lucy, and another whose name I do not know, sit attentively at the foot of the bed. They talk to us, at first too quietly for anybody to hear above Amy's screams, describing Elowen's position, head out, then shoulders. Amid her agony, legs propped up and splayed apart by supports, in a gap between her deep and fatigued breathing, Amy asks the question, *What is this all for? She's dead.*

It cuts through the room.

With one final expulsion of breath and heave of her whole body, Amy collapses forward, throwing her head back into the pillow as Elowen is born. I dare not look over the blue paper screen, but I can see the two midwives leaning forward, looking and holding our daughter who must be warm, but without a heartbeat. I wonder what does she look like.

Then silence.

It's 1.35 a.m on the 27th July, 2017.

I lay my head on Amy's chest and close my eyes.

*

I wake to Lucy, the midwife who delivered Elowen, walking over to Amy who is sat upright on the hospital bed in a deep sleep. She's in the same position as when she went to sleep, facing me, her mouth slightly open. Tears brim into my eyes when I look at her.

The lights come on. They are stark and bright, one flickers. I sit up, almost embarrassed that she saw me sleeping. I make sure that the blanket is pulled over me.

Amy stirs when Lucy stands besides her bed, saying *Amy, Amy,* in almost a whisper. Amy opens her eyes and turns her head round to face Lucy. She shuffles further up the bed, but finds it painful. Her skin is so pale. There are dark circles around her eyes.

I squeeze Amy's hand then go to the bathroom. It seems that it is still dark outside, the high buildings of the hospital blocking out the morning light. I dare not look in the mirror.

Obeying the pull to be close to Amy, I sit back down on the bed and lie down. My mind is empty, like a hollow shell. My skin aches. While Lucy checks over Amy, taking her blood pressure, breathing and heart rate, another person enters wheeling in a trolley, offering breakfast. Neither of us can eat. We drink water, that is all.

Lucy guides Amy up the bed, as do I, holding her arm, helping her to shift further up. With the bed cover over the part of her stomach, Lucy pulls on blue plastic gloves and kneels down at the end of the bed. She is pleased that Amy, despite a tear that required three stitches soon after Elowen's birth, hasn't suffered excessive physical damage. Amy lies back down, slowly, and with care.

Before Lucy leaves she tells us that Elowen weighed seven pounds and five ounces. I find it hard to catch my breath. Amy closes her eyes and turns her head away. I nod back at Lucy. She smiles wistfully and leaves.

Seven pounds and five ounces, Amy and I say together.

That's perfect, I add.

We ask if they know why she died. Nothing abnormal, they say, although the cord was wrapped very tightly around her.

As the doors swing open I glimpse Nina walking fast past and wonder when she'll come to see us. I hear the cries of a baby nearby, soon muffled once the doors swing closed. I do not wish to hear anything beyond these doors.

I wait in anticipation for Amy's movements, and hang on for any words she may muster up the strength to say. I feel nothing. I cannot process what has happened, and is happening. I do not even try. There is no energy for it. There is only energy for me to attend to Amy, my sole focus, which is happening of its own accord. I simply fall in line.

Amy wants a shower – she can still taste vomit in her mouth. She was sick repeatedly before falling asleep, and I held out a cardboard container to catch what quickly became heavy and soggy. I wiped her mouth in a daze before she fell asleep.

I press the red button behind Amy's bed. A nurse enters. A new face. She says very little, and helps Amy off the bed with me beside her, hands at the ready. The shower comes on. Water splatters onto a huge, blue birthing ball that I had stowed away in here, and bounces off against the mirror, the walls, us, soaking the whole bathroom. Carefully removing Amy's hospital gown, and rolling the ball out of the shower tray, we step in under the warm water together. I wash her hair, and her body. She is so tender, precious. I am glad to be taking care of her. Even now, somehow, she manages a faint smile as we embrace beneath the shower, just like we do at home. Because I have been so used to not embracing Amy too tightly, keeping my stomach back from hers, not putting pressure on Elowen, it feels very strange to be able to touch my tummy to hers. It's no longer heavy and tight. That space, reserved for Elowen, has gone.

Another midwife visits, reassuring us that we'll be OK, praising Amy for her bravery and how well she did to push Elowen out. She informs us that at 11 a.m. we will be relocated to another room, where we'll be able to spend time with Elowen in a quieter part of the hospital, a place specifically for the bereaved parents.

Amy and I lie together on the narrow bed. She falls in and out of sleep. My mind is blank. I stare, my head resting on Amy's shoulder. I stare and look around the room, taking nothing in.

At 9 a.m. a senior doctor enters, holding a thin file of papers. *I am sorry*, she says, taking a seat on a blue plastic chair besides the bed. We are sat up now.

I am so sorry to do this, she continues, *but I have some important questions to ask about what you would like us to do with… What's the baby's name?*

Amy says nothing.

Elowen, I say. *Her name is Elowen.* A powerful sense of anguish overcomes me when I say her name.

That's a lovely name, the doctor replies.

Thank you, Amy and I say together, proudly.

We are so deep in the moment of saying her name that the doctor's initial question catches us off guard. I watch her go through a series of papers, before stopping at one over which her pen hovers.

Some parents decide to donate their child's organs to research, towards helping understanding the causes of stillbirth and if we want a post mortem.

There is a long pause after she says this. I hold onto Amy's hand. The doctor seems in a hurry to get the form completed, repeatedly glancing back at the door, pulling down her sleeve to look at her watch.

Yes, I think we would like to donate her organs for research, Amy says, put on the spot. *We would hate for this to happen to anyone else,* I continue, without thinking.

The doctor puts pen to paper. It seems like the right thing to do. We stare ahead. I feel so cold. After the doctor leaves, we lay back down. Everything will be OK, because soon we will get to meet our little girl.

Amy eats a little, as do I. Family visit. The morning passes. Eleven. Noon. One.

It is not until around 4 p.m. that a midwife comes in and tells us that the new room is ready. Family help us pack our things, then walk with us. We keep our heads down. I lift mine only once, at the sight – seen through the rectangular window of a door – of a mum holding her newborn baby, swaddled in white blankets. A man is smiling over them, and stroking the baby's face. Around them stands a circle of family and friends.

My mum and Amy's mum go in the lift with us. When the doors open, a midwife is waiting for us. I think she's the midwife who brought in the Memory Box yesterday evening.

Our family go into a separate room while Amy and I are led through double doors into a space that is very unlike the standard hospital room. There is a double bed. Lamps on bedside tables. A patterned duvet and navy-blue throw. A television on a cream-yellow shelf, bookended by DVDs. Thick, dark green curtains are half drawn across a large window with a view out across suburbs: towers, Southampton Docks, derricks, ships, and the New Forest – home – in the hazy, summer distance. The midwife is stood behind us, as quiet as a shadow.

Besides the bed is a cot. Empty, and pushed close to the bedside, up near the pillows. I do not understand why there is an empty cot in our room. Amy turns to the midwife and asks for her to remove it, which she does. We watch her leave, then sit down on the edge of the bed.

What was all that about? I ask. Amy says nothing. She hangs her head low. I stand and close the curtains.

I do not know why but it hasn't occurred to me to ask why we haven't seen Elowen all day. We go along with what's happening, with very little to say. Around 5 p.m., the same midwife knocks and comes in. She asks if we would like to see our daughter, or to look through photographs first before meeting her in person.

The midwife waits in the room while we decide. I'm shivering with a fear similar to the fear of seeing Elowen being born lifeless, our longed-for daughter quiet on the table. I have never known feelings like this. My mouth is dry. My stomach twinges with a dull pain. When I say, *The photographs first, please,* my jaw shakes, and nausea roils through me.

We sit up at the head of the bed, with the pillows behind us. My arm is around Amy, her head on my chest. We wait.

The midwife knocks and enters, carrying a white envelope which she sets down upon the bedside table next to me. I stare at the blank envelope before opening it. I then look away. The movement I have to make in order to pick up the envelope feels like a monumental task. Amy lifts her head off mine, and reaches over. We both sit up, and I hold one side of the envelope while Amy holds the other. She lifts the envelope flap, and I can see the very tops of the photographs, a blur of colours.

I then take out the first photograph, carefully, as if holding Elowen for the first time. It is a photograph of a hand. Small, pudgy, creased. Palm up. Her right hand. The little fingers of the hands are curled over slightly as though another hand had held it and very recently let go. The shapes of the fingernails are perfect, clear as glass.

We burst into tears, and then an overwhelming feeling like happiness but bigger overcomes us. Our daughter's hand. Elowen's hand. The fear subsides. I take out the next photograph. A pair of feet, crossed over, delicate and yet strong, creased soles and the little mounds of the ankles, the toes. A yellow blanket laid over, just above the ankles. I am in awe. I want to see other photographs.

We arrange them in a crescent on the bed. I can't take my eyes off them. We pick them up, one at a time, and pass them to one another.

Her face, I say. *Look at her face, and her nose, her cheeks.* I pass the photo to Amy, who then hands me another of her face, but this time taken from a different angle, on her right side, pink cheeks, mouth slightly pursed open, lips plump, ready to make sounds, big eyes closed in sleep, the perfect curved lines of the eyelashes.

She is sleeping. Yes, she is sleeping, that's all. And I can see the lobes of her ears. I can see exactly what it would be like if she opened her eyes, looked at me, and smiled. And I see that face far into the future, on mornings when I wake her for school, on walks in the woods when she looks back at me, hiding behind an oak tree, swimming with in the waves, running along the beach, clutching my hands, her mother's hands. Far into the future my heart has gone to wait for my daughter, and is also here now, in fear, and beating with love. There's no such thing as time. Tears fall on the photographs. Amy's and mine.

There's a knock at the door.

The midwife pops her head round. I press my eyes with my fingertips, wipe my nose with the back of my hand.

Would you like to see her now? she says, politely.

Amy and I look at one another.

Yes, we say. *Yes. Thank you,* I add.

I suggest, she softly adds, *that you don't remove her woolen hat as her head wont have gone back into shape after the birth.*

To ready ourselves, I gather the photographs together and place them back, carefully, into the envelope, which Amy takes and puts on her bedside table. We sit on the edge of the bed. We stare at the door, and wait.

A cot enters first, pushed towards us on wheels across the room that, suddenly, feels large and spacious. The midwife leaves the cot, side on to us, a few feet away. She walks out. It is slightly too far away to see directly in, which means I cannot see Elowen. I need to stand up first and bring it closer, but find it hard. We stay seated, the cot remote from us. I get nearer to Amy, shoulder against shoulder. I am terrified. Something is holding me back, urging me not to see.

I rise, and just like seeing the first photograph, I am pulled towards her as though caught by a tide. Her presence, even before seeing her, floods the room. I stand up and take one step towards the cot, glimpse her cheek, her nose, the fresh colour of her pure skin, the shape of her body asleep and tucked beneath the daffodil-yellow blanket. She becomes the world.

Drawn closer, and without hesitation, I place my hands gently on the rim of the cot, and lean into her, into her presence. Careful not to disturb her, I gaze in reverential silence. I am stunned. Amy finds herself on the other side of the cot, directly opposite me. I do not come up for air because I breathe her in. We both breathe her in, again and again, and yet still we are not too close as to wake her, break the spell of sleep. My mind tells me that she needs to sleep because, like her mum, she's been through a lot the past few days. Her rest is everything. When she is properly rested, then we will be able to scoop her up in our arms, and fuss, and rock, and hold her. But my heart, or whatever it is in me now that speaks of things I do not quite understand knows that our daughter *seems* to sleep. And yet, I still do not wish to disturb her. So I go on gazing until, at last, I pluck up the courage to bring my lips to the bridge of her nose. A kiss. Eyes to eyes. Mine open, hers closed. They are like eggshells in cups of shadow, concealing their colours, their light.

I close my eyes and concentrate on the kiss — not so much a kiss as a rest from pain, a reprieve from time, a suspension of everything I have ever known or thought I knew. A breathing space of pure air. And so, with my lips resting on the skin of her nose, just below her eyes, I inhale her again, filling my lungs, my body, with a scent which brings to mind a waterfall, Cwm Idwal, in the Glyderau mountains of northern Snowdonia. A blast and roar of clear water over granite rock, cutting its way through the narrow mountain pass, plunging into the lake below with ceaseless, billowings of spray. The image a waterfall ends. I cannot breathe in anymore.

Opening my eyes on her again, I lift away as carefully as I leant down. Amy is leaning, too, over the side of the cot, gazing, lost in the world of her daughter. I kneel down beside Amy, wrap my arm around her.

To think that parents gaze down, and scoop up, embrace, their living child, seems nothing short of miraculous. The mother and father whom I saw on my way here, the other parents whose children were born in the night. Those parents. How do they feel? What do they see?

After some time, I cannot say how long, I lift up the phone that is beside the TV and tell the midwife to let our waiting families in.

Amy's mum, dad, sister, step-dad and step-mum. My dad, my mum. They all enter the room, quietly, one at a time, moving gently to meet their granddaughter and niece.

Amy and I are sat together on the edge of the bed, with Elowen, in her cot, pulled closed to us. Waves of pride come over me when the grandparents first see her, and then, one at a time, bend low to either kiss her, gaze, or stroke her face. The silence that comes over the room when they meet her is not like the gut-wrenching silence of the hospital room at her birth – a room absent of a child's first screams and cries. In this gathered hush, the presence of Elowen quietly fills our hearts. But at some point, the spell is broken – I think someone spoke of something other than Elowen – and I begin to feel uncomfortable, rising to my feet, and moving away from Elowen. A quick current of panicked thoughts runs through me.

There is a dead child in the room. There is a dead child in the room. My daughter is dead. My daughter is dead, here in this room, and we are all just stood or sat doing nothing. Everyone has to leave. They have to leave. I have to have it back how it was. Me, Amy, Elowen. Please, everyone, just leave, leave. I want to go back.

When everyone does leave, I find myself at the back of the room. And, with the last close of the door, I sit back down with Amy. I feel less uncomfortable in my skin again. The chill that overcame me in the crowd of loving, well-meaning family members, abates.

The small body in the cot besides us becomes less of a dead child again, turning from a cold and faraway shape of perished innocence, into the presence of our daughter. She has my full attention. I do not want to be distracted again.

Later, we shower, one at a time, so as not to leave Elowen alone in the room. I hear Amy weeping. Her eyes are bloodshot when she steps back into the room. I look at her with a deep sense of longing for things to be OK, happy, even, like any other parent's first day with their child. But we are not those parents. This is us: inside a sorrow that was unimaginable a few days ago.

Amy's skin is warm and damp from the shower when I hold her against me. I breathe in the scent of her dark, wet hair. All the while, Amy is looking over my shoulder, at our daughter asleep. I am desperate for Amy to be OK. But I do not know what that means and what awaits us, or what we will have to face. I simply hold her as she looks on, a mother to her child.

*

My eyes open, blurred by sleep, on the colour pink. I hear a voice, a male voice. The vision begins to clear as I sit up. Amy is awake, sat up beside me in bed. The obstetrician, doing his morning rounds, wearing a tight pink shirt, is talking to Amy, asking if she is feeling OK, physically. There is blood on the sheets where Amy lay, but only a little. The doctor scribbles down notes on a clipboard, rehanging it on the wooden rail at the foot of the bed. He leaves, the clack of his polished shoes on the floor heard down the hallway even after the doors close, a junior doctor scurries along beside him.

I lean over, expecting to see Elowen asleep, or fidgeting in her cot, trembling as she yawns, eyelids fluttering open, waking to demand a feed. But she is not there, neither is the cot. *Where is she? Where is she?* Then I begin to recall that the midwife came in around 9 p.m., to take Elowen away because sleep was beginning to take hold of us, especially Amy. I have taken 5 mg of Valium prescribed by the doctor earlier in the day.

It seemed right that she should be looked after in another room while we rested, but this morning the guilt of having fallen asleep during our first night as parents is crushing.

Amy and I rise together and get changed. But what do we do now? Do we gather our belongings? Are we going to see her again? Are we going home today?

There's a loud knock on the door and a heavy-set man enters, distraught, tears rolling down his cheeks. He says that he's with his wife in the room next door and doesn't understand why his baby, a boy, died in the night. He wants answers from the doctors. Why, when his son was born, was the umbilical cord wrapped and coiled around his neck so tightly that his little face was blue and his body limp? *Why*, he keeps on saying. *Why?*

He stops talking and clenches his dark hair in both of his big hands. The agony he feels is palpable, and I do not know what to say except *I am sorry*. He then goes on to explain how his wife cannot let their son go, how she wants to bathe him and stay longer in the hospital just to be with him. He takes a breath, closing his eyes. *I am so sorry*, I say again. *I am so sorry*.

Amy is stood behind me. I can tell she is anxious to leave the room to go and see Elowen, wherever she may be – not far, we hope, not far – and so I open the door to encourage the man to step out into the hallway. I follow him out. Not knowing what to say or do, I take out a thin book from a bookcase on the wall, and rip out the front page. I write down my name and number. He takes the paper, folds it carefully in half, and holds onto it. He opens the door of his room, and steps in, without another word or look my way. As the door slowly closes I glimpse him, for a moment, stood before his wife who is cradling their baby boy. She is gazing down at him. Their son held tight against her bare chest.

When I turn around to go back into our room to Amy, there's a woman talking to her. Amy is sitting on the edge of the bed. Our hospital bag beside her.

Hi, Will, the woman says in a soft voice. *I am so sorry for your loss. What a beautiful girl you have, the most beautiful I have ever seen in this hospital, if you don't mind me saying, a right corker! And her name, too, Elowen, so pretty. What does it mean?*

It means Elm Tree in Cornish, I say, with a lump in my throat, still standing until I sit down beside Amy, feeling for the edge of the bed with my right hand, not letting my eyes lose sight on the conversation unfolding in case I miss some piece of critically important news.

I am a bereavement midwife. She says her name but I forget it instantly. *It's my job to see that Elowen is being properly looked after, and that you two, as her parents, are being taken care of.* She sighs, then continues. *There are, however, a number of questions I need to ask you, and things I need to tell you.* She folds her hands in her lap, and looks down. I am reminded of the doctor yesterday morning that came into our room just as we woke up, asking what we wanted to do with Elowen's organs.

There's a quiet pause before she speaks, clearing her throat. The clock on the wall ticks. *Have you had any thoughts on funeral arrangements? And you must, also, register Elowen in the coming weeks. I would recommend sooner rather than later. I am happy to book in the appointment for you.*

The question of her funeral rams me into a corner. My heart gallops. My hands tremble. I feel breathless, my throat constricted. There is no way out of this. In blind anger I turn away and grab the nearest object, a lampshade, and crush it in my hands, the glass bulb cracks and breaks. I rip the cable straight out from the plug and dash the stand against the floor. I pull my head into hands.

There's a moment of silence in which I immediately regret what I have done, the shame of it making me cower my head. I lift the lamp back up, slowly, as the bereavement midwife says she understands and that she can't even imagine what we're going through. Amy offers to pay for a new lamp. The midwife refuses. She doesn't want to be asking these questions, she explains, but the pressure is on in such a busy hospital, to keep things moving. There's only a restricted allowance of time, care and attention, even in circumstance like ours. When we can't even muster the energy to eat, there is this pressure for us to make decisions about our daughter. I feel deeply wronged, though there is no one I can blame.

I'm sorry, we haven't given her funeral any thought at all, Amy says, consoling me. *And does Elowen not get a birth certificate? Why do we have to do this so soon?* she asks.

The midwife is apologetic, and knowing she won't get any answers from us, she takes notes on a pile of papers that were wedged between her outer hip and the chair. She explains that a baby's death must be registered in person, by one or both parents, at a register office, then a

Stillbirth Certificate can be issued. In England and Wales, this has to be done within six weeks of the baby's birth. In Scotland, it must be done within three weeks. She goes on to explain various options for the funeral: cremation, burial, woodland burial. We hear what she is saying, but her words fall down into the space between us, droplets of sound, like moulten lead at the bottom of the sea.

I cannot fathom why we have to go through the logistics of the funeral and certificate right now, when all we yearn to do is hold Elowen. Suddenly, overwhelmingly, I want to go home. Where else is there to go? There is this urgent need to return to something familiar, to get away from the hospital, where I know my dogs will run to greet me with the touch of their fur and the happy wags. I want to see them. I wonder if they are OK without us. But I cannot go home without Elowen.

Because, the midwife goes on, *parts of Elowen will go to research, the funeral may be delayed, but not by a lot, perhaps by a week or so. You will get a call in the coming days to make arrangements, and to register Elowen as a stillbirth.*

As a stillbirth? I ask. *Not a birth? Not a death?*

I don't even expect an answer.

I just want to see Elowen, and tell her everything will be OK.

We open the door with consideration, stepping through, Amy first, then me, just as we might at home, taking the lightest of steps and the quietest of breaths so as not to wake her.

There she is, in the centre of the room, in the cold cot. I move around her, almost in circles, cautiously moving nearer with each step, until I stop entirely, and bend down to gaze at her face. Amy steps in beside me. The preciousness of our daughter is overwhelming, more so than the brutal fact of her death. The beauty of her, the milk-white cheeks, the closed eyes, and the woollen hat and blanket tucked in around her, and those hands that I think I can see moving. Her presence, like apple blossom, fills every space in me. I will never know what she looks like with her eyes open, only what she looks like when asleep.

My daughter. What can I do now? Can you hear me? Did you hear my voice when you were in your mum? I know you. I know you from all that I have felt, all that I have seen, and heard, and touched. It seems like I have arrived at you after a long time, which stretches way back before me, as if all my life has been about falling into the thread that connects me to you, and you to me. And now here you are. And I don't know what to do, except kiss you softly.

So I kiss her nose, and cheek, and forehead. And I am not conscious of a goodbye because this is not truly happening, I am not here. I can't be. I am unsure of everything, except her beauty.

The door closes on her, and we step out into the bright hallway, where nurses and midwives and doctors walk to and fro, and patients linger or talk to one another. We walk through them, heads hidden, our eyes blinkered, to the lift that takes us down, down, down.

Amy waits with her mum and dad and sister while I go to find the car, but I don't know which way to go, so I walk back to Amy, unable to leave. Amy's sister passes me a chocolate bar, and I unwrap it quickly, mechanically, and eat.

*

This morning, Amy's dad drives us to the registration of Elowen's death. Not birth. I sit in the back seat with Amy and Amy's mum. My mum is in the passenger seat.

Arriving at the registration offices – stark brick buildings clustered together on the outskirts of Southampton – I step out of the car and sit with Amy on a bench in the shade of a chestnut tree. We shelter from the smoke and roar of traffic, the punishing glare of the sun, the crowds of people laughing or busy walking alone, their ears plugged with headphones, their footsteps full of intent.

Out from the double doors comes a happy family, pushing their newborn in a pram straight towards us, and then another family, and another. There are no allowances made here for parents like us. Why isn't there another door we could go through, or another appointment time, which doesn't bring us face to face with this?

At 11 a.m. we go through the double doors, Amy and I behind our family. A woman with curly blonde hair, looking at us over the rim of her glasses, leads us down a long corridor into a far office. She sits down behind a wide desk. We sit down too, Amy and I facing her, our family on chairs along the wall.

The questions begin.

Name? she says, *of deceased person.*

A lump in my throat clears, and I say *Elowen.* My voice trembles.

How do I spell that? she replies, expressionless, never taking her eyes off the computer screen, typing our answers into the computer.

E L O W E N, Amy says.

You're going to have to say that a little louder please, I couldn't hear you, she says sharply.

I feel cold.

Again, Amy and I say together, *ELOWEN.*

Occupation? she asks.

Ummm, hostel owner, I reply, my lips weakened after having to spell out her name.

I want this to end. But it goes on and on and on.

The drive home seems long, down the same route we drove to the hospital. The engine clunks and grinds. Our car breaks down just as we reach home. Amy's dad organises for it to be towed.

Amy and I go for walk out on the heath with the dogs. It cheers me to see them run through the heather. The sun, however, is too bright. Swallows dart overhead in a broken flurry of ones, two and threes. I watch them for no longer than they take to pass. I look but do not see. The sky darkens suddenly under passing cloud, and my eyes feel more at rest in shadow. My hand feels at rest in Amy's. When she speaks, my ears feel at rest in Amy's voice.

What is this world, where our daughter is not near? How can I live in a place like this? Everything is strange and cruel and wrong. This is not the life I have known. I am somewhere and someone else now. And yet, and yet, there is still Amy beside me. And our dogs, their paws drumming on the hard, summer ground.

At last, the call comes from the funeral directors that we can go see Elowen at the Chapel of Rest. I am told that two weeks have passed since seeing her in hospital. A post-mortem was undertaken, although the results won't come through for at least six months.

I am filled with excitement to be seeing our daughter. *We can finally bring her home* a voice in me says. She will be so happy to see us, to hear our voices, our touch and smell. *She has missed us,* I say to Amy. Before we leave, I go up to her room to make sure it's all ready. *Will she remember us? Where has she been for the past two weeks?*

After the fluster to park the car, and paying for an all-day ticket, we walk down Eastleigh high street. The funeral directors comes into view, sandwiched between a hairdressers and a toy shop. The front window is tinted, throwing back our reflections. I knock on the door. No answer. I knock again. A man opens the door wide. He has tattoos that are spread up both sides of his neck and along his bare forearms. His sleeves are tightly rolled into untidy rings at his elbows.

Come in, he says.

The room is mostly red: a crimson carpet and pale red walls. The air is thick with the overpowering fragrance of rose.

She'll be with you shortly, he says, gesturing towards a bench. He smiles then leaves down a hallway, going through a white door which closes just slowly enough for me to glimpse a white room with white tables. I am nervous, my mouth is dry.

A young lady comes into the room through another door. She smiles, and her smile and eyes have a real tenderness.

After an exchange of niceties, which I am eager to finish, she says *Elowen is this way. I hope you like her room. I hope it's OK. She is the most beautiful baby we have ever seen. You should be so proud.*

Standing up from the bench, we follow her down the hallway and stop by a yellow door. The woman steps back, letting Amy go first. She turns the handle slowly. My nerves get the better of me and I stall, breathe deeply, then walk inside. Just like when I finally broke through and saw the first photographs of Elowen, my nerves subside and my heart lifts when I see her at the far end of the room, snug in her cot, surrounded by some of the things we got for her.

Don't worry, Mummy and Daddy are here.

We enter quietly, but do not go straight to her. I hear the door faintly click shut behind us. The room is warm. The scent of rose too strong, lit candles on either side of a shelf above her steady after a brief flicker caused by the open door. Amy rushes over and picks her up straight away, and holds her to her heart. Then she places her down again as if laying her down for sleep. We sit down on chairs, side by side, about two metres away from her. A blanket is folded over her, and tucked in around the shape of her body. A yellow woollen hat casts a pale shadow over her face, her closed eyes. Her beauty fills me with warmth.

I am so glad to see you again, Elowen. It's your Mummy and Daddy here. We love you so much.

I have a hard time keeping my tears at bay.

Then, together, we go to her. And together we are with her as any other parent would be with their baby as it sleeps. When the time is right, we will lift her out of the cot and hold her and talk to her and stroke her face and cup her little feet and hands in our hands. But not yet, not quite yet.

We have brought a few more things with us to place around her – things from her room, or which we bought for her in the weeks running up to her birth. Now we put them in carefully chosen places, as though at an altar. The little wooden spoon I carved from alder wood, with her name engraved on the handle. A sprig of heather tugged from the heath at home. A fat green acorn pulled from her oak tree. A photograph of Amy and I, taken by my mum a month before at the beach, the two of us clambering out of the sea, me helping Amy tread free from the waves, happiness written on our faces. And there's a photograph of Daisy and Dilly.

Amy scoops her up. I watch her hold her daughter. Both loves of my life. Then she passes me Elowen. Her weight in my arms is indescribable. I do not want this to end.

*

Over the course of the next three days we spend every moment we can with her, and the funeral directors say we can spend longer, but on the final afternoon it somehow feels as if it's time. Amy says Elowen's skin is greying. We hold her cold feet until the day's end. We place her in her cot, surrounded and kept company by all her things.

The door is closing. There is a thick scent of rose.

Bye bye, Elowen, I love you.

The door is closed.

Outside, it is warm and bright. I almost step off the high kerb and fall straight into oncoming traffic.

Amy goes into the toyshop next door. I tell her not to. I lean on a bin and wait. She comes out with gifts for my niece whose birthday is in a few days.

We walk down the street side by side, through crowds, find the car in the parking lot and then we just drive away. We drive away, forever.

*

I wake to rain pattering and scraping at the bedroom window, and a wind skittering around the outside of the cottage. Sunlight comes and goes, then returns half an hour later when Amy, Daisy, Dilly and I leave the house. Amy's mum watches us leave. We cannot be late.

Elowen will be cremated at 9 a.m. But we will not be with her. The funeral directors will be with her. We decided that we could not bear to be there. I don't know if this is the right or wrong thing to do, all I know is that we're getting ready to leave and walk out to her oak tree.

In my jacket pocket I have a box of matches, two tea lights and two candles. Amy has the photo of her lying on her left side, my hand upon her shoulder. The same knitted yellow blanket is pulled up just past her mouth, almost touching her button nose. The faded pink and white knitted hat covers her head, and ends just above her big, closed eyes. Her skin is warm-looking, healthy.

Out on the heath, away from the sheltering arm of the woods, the wind builds and billows, the heather is tugged this way and that, puddles ripple, and splash as we walk through them. The sun is gone. The clouds darken. The air is cool. Ponies gather on the dark horizon. A crow battles south, into the wind. A storm in August.

Amy and I hold hands all the way to the oak, which comes into sight once we veer off the open heath and follow a deer track towards the woods. Scots pines come into view, their buckled tops roaring in the wind. Elowen's Oak stands out on its own, between heath and wood. The branches reach low. The leaves rattle. It begins to rain, but the rain is blown away from us, showering across our view.

It's 8.45. I gather fallen branches from the tree and stack them into a low square. I place the candles carefully within the square. Amy brings out her photograph and secures it between the branches, facing it towards us so we can see her and she can see us.

Dilly has taken her place beside a silver birch, lying, looking up at us in that way of hers that says *why aren't we walking*? I laugh a little when I catch sight of Daisy, who has managed to balance a long stick perfectly across the back of her neck. She catches my eye with a look of happy bewilderment.

Amy and I sit cross-legged. The ground is wet. Rain comes and goes. I strike a match within the square of branches, but the wind blows it out immediately. On the third attempt, just as the wind slackens, and with the help of Amy's hands protecting the flame, the candles are lit. The flames are blown to and fro, but they hold, anchored on their blackening wicks. I quickly run over to the edge of the heath and snap away a small length of purple heather, and place it in front of her photograph, along with a green acorn I yank from a branch dangling above us. Rain spills from the big leaves, which rise with an old slowness, rather than spring back up.

We were told that the funeral directors would read her a story, along with something Amy had written and placed beside her in her cot. Amy had asked them yesterday to cover her face with a blanket, so she couldn't see the flames.

Amy unfolds a piece of paper, a copy of what she had written, and together we read aloud the same words.

Dear Elowen,
Mummy and Daddy are with you on the start of your journey home
to us today and in a few days you'll be in our arms again. When this
is read to you we will be walking to Mummy and Daddy's favourite
oak tree and thinking of you every second. You are so loved. You are
so wanted. You are the best thing that ever happened to us.
We love you, Elowen.

It's just passed 9 a.m.

Elowen has been cremated. Her body has left the world.

We sit with her photograph for a long while, until the tea lights extinguish themselves in small pools of rainwater and wax, and the larger candles shed even more wax into the earth.

A deep emptiness rises, like a sinkhole. I feel a tightness in my chest and chills in my gut. Something is about to happen, something is beginning.

Amy and I hold onto one another as the wind kicks up and the rain is blown towards us. The sky is very dark. The huge clouds that were gathering earlier in the morning have now amassed, and do not move. The candles are blown out. I place them back into my jacket pocket. I also lace the stack of oak branches back below the trunk. There is a pool of hardened wax on the earth. I look at it and leave it there.

Amy takes her photograph and holds it gently against the oak, up on the wide saddle, at about head height, where the first, big branches divide and diverge. We face her and tell her we love her.

*

Hearing a car crunch and scrape on our gravel drive the following morning, Amy and I go outside. Amy's mum and dad are in the house. My parents are coming over later. Mum says she has made us dinner.

The car slowly approaches. I lean on the timber gate in the sun. Amy stands beside me. The car comes to a gentle halt. It is the two women who looked after Elowen in the Chapel of Rest, and who were with

Elowen during the cremation. They were the last people to be with her. It was one of them that read her a story – *Guess how much I love you.*

Why does my mind always go to Elowen in the fire? I close my eyes as a way of not seeing the image, but feel the heat of the flames.

One of the ladies is holding the teddy bear. She brings it forward, and Amy takes it into her arms. It's about the size of a baby and weighted with Elowen's ashes, which are kept secure in a pocket in the bear's back. Amy holds it tight. We say goodbye to the funeral directors.

An empty space is filled when I take the bear in my arms, and hold it close to my chest. The size feels familiar and comforting. But I know the weight of the ashes is not all of Elowen.

When my mum arrives she holds the bear. My dad and Amy's dad say nothing, but share looks of sorrow. In the evening, after an endless day, we watch a movie with the bear between us, and eat chocolate.

At some point after the movie has finished, we softly sing Elowen's lullaby, *Baby Els, Baby E-LO-WEN...* Amy weeps and I get in as close as possible to her with the softness of the bear between us. Together, by lamplight, we take out the ashes, which are kept in a small green bag sewn shut. I move the bag through my fingers, hold it between my hands. Together, we put the ashes back into the bear and lay it down again between us.

Amy closes her eyes.

III

Running

In the absence of light
I focus on outlines.
I cannot directly look at things
otherwise they blur,
the leaves, branches, her.
So I look at the periphery, edges.
One upheaval at a time,
Until dark trees are rendered visible.

One more adjustment to the dark.

I am standing at the front gate. There are stars in the sky. There are two figures in front of me. Two New Forest ponies nose to nose. I slowly count them, as though I'm learning to count, *one, two*.

Darkness everywhere.

I count the animals again. *One, two. There are two horses.*

I can now hear their deep breathing, the gentle squeeze of bellows, each exhale rises like smoke into the night sky.

I can see a bit more clearly. There are things outside of me, like two ponies. I am not sure what to make of all this wreckage. Where is there to go?

One, two. Two horses. I see where I am now. The house is behind me. It hasn't left. Amy is inside, and I am just where I was a minute ago. I grip the gate, or my hand grips the gate. I look down at my arms and they feel alien to me, as detached from me as this evening sky, the ground, the trees. I turn again to the ponies. I watch where their breath goes, and then my eyes are caught by a star brighter than all the rest. My eyes rest on it.

Elowen arrives gently at my lips, like rope thrown to a raft. But I cannot say it, take it. If I say it, I don't know what will happen. I am terrified.

If I take her name where will I go?

What will happen if I say her name?

I turn from looking at the star and direct my gaze down to my hands which are still holding the top bar of the gate. I grip as hard as I can. I clench my teeth as hard as I can. I have never felt fury like this, a white hot rage .

Fuck it all. I fucking hate you. I fucking hate you.

Words falter.

The shout comes through me so hard its hurts my throat. It overtakes me. I crave violence. Wherever I look there is the world still going on without her, and I do not see how I am meant to find a foothold. Nothing, there is nothing. I feel nothing, then blown apart, wrenched down, pinned. I can hardly breathe. *My daughter, my daughter.*

I pick up a large paving slab from the side of the outbuilding and throw it against the brickwork, as hard as I can. Then again, and again. The brickwork has cracked, the stone slab is in pieces on the ground. I scream.

The ponies bolt. Amy runs out of the cottage, wrapping her arms around me as I fall, digging my fingers sharply into my head, tearing at my skull. There is blood on my fingertips.

It's been like this for a while now – since the hospital.

But when was that?

This cycle of darkness, burial, then some vague sense of emerging, clambering out towards a world I once knew. Or someone else called *me* once knew. Then a falling back in, breath taken. Dragged through ashes and dust.

In this movement I look constantly for Amy. The anchor, the root, the harbour, the hand I can hold at the end of it all. We are trying not to drift apart as we did in the weeks immediately after Elowen's death. I in my world of pain, she in hers. And, then, we suddenly found one another again. Or more likely, something greater and darker allowed us to go towards one another again.

I have to get to her, get closer. I cannot get caught in the rip tide of my own personal grief. Even my mum, noticing how consumed I am, pulls me to one side and tells me Elowen was not only mine, but Amy's too, and reminds me that Amy had her in her body and gave birth to her. Sometimes I forget this. I am ashamed that I do.

All we have now is a teddy bear with her ashes inside.

Fire and ashes.

My mind – not mine at all but something else ripping through me – peers at the images of her cremation, repeatedly, ending with her little body in the flames. I cannot bear to think of it. Fire gets into my head at any moment. And the guilt of not being with her. Why were we not with her? We were at her oak, that's why. Yes, that's right, we were there at the tree. Is that enough? Did we do all that we could?

Elowen, where are you?

The Valium helps me to sleep. But I wake still, hearing her imagined cries coming from her room. And beside me, Amy cries. I watch Amy sleeping sometimes, her peace of forgetfulness until morning comes when we rise quietly, when words don't do anything for us, said or read. The only word that means something is *Elowen*. So we say that, as often as we breathe it seems. The touch of a hand helps, the lightness of fingers, or an embrace into one another's shoulders as we pass each other on the landing or stand in the open doorway of Elowen's nursery. Walking side by side helps, Amy and me, our feet moving in time across the fields, stopping to thumb away a tear from a cold cheek, taking turns to stroke the damp eyelids.

Family come and go, making us meals, doing all they can. And when they leave there is me and Amy and the bear, Daisy and Dilly.

She is here, still, surely. Our daughter can't just simply leave the world.

I can't wait to finally hold her, see her.

We believe that we are going her hold her again soon.

The stacks of unused nappies, the empty cot we cannot bear to disassemble and put away, the monitor that I chose and learned to use. The lines of bottles on the shelves, the books even, the clothes that Amy so lovingly chose, the excitement as we both held up outfits in the aisles of shops. *Yes, that one*, I would say about a pair of dungarees, or a summer hat, a pair of shoes. That yellow dress, bright in my mind like the sun.

All the bright paraphernalia we carefully chose on those days out in the shops. The rucksack and the sling I couldn't wait to swaddle her in to take her out into the woods.

She will never hear the summer birdsong, see the swallows flick free from the wire. The things I wanted to show her. The thrum of nightjars, their churr, now only announces, repeatedly and relentlessly, her parting. And yet she has not parted. She is here, surely. The feel of the long grass in our field, the shape of the oak tree and the ash tree at its far end. I look at these things and my dreams of taking her to them have not yet faded; they are as strong as they were before she was born. And my dreams persist, the dreams I had for her and me and us before she was born, the dreams born in the nine months of waiting, expecting. But she's not here to complete them.

I find Amy now and again holding her tender belly. She says she can still feel the kicks, the phantom jostling and thumps. I place my hand there hoping to feel them too.

I find Amy stroking her stretch marks, too, running her forefinger along their patterns, tracing the traces of her baby, the traces of Elowen, the girl that has vanished.

Sometimes, I stand in Elowen's room, the sunlight playing on the grey walls through parted curtains embroidered with animal and forest scenes, and imagine cradling Elowen, feeling her weight in my arms. I close my arms, and we drift into one another. My girl, my one and only girl. I kneel.

She is everywhere. And nowhere. Everywhere, nowhere.

*

I don't think Amy and I can get through this alone. We need help. After searching the internet for someone who specialises in child-bereavement, our first appointment with a counsellor will, we hope, offer some kind of guidance, or at least a witness to our loss.

Heathland opens up on either side of the road. Along the verges, wild ponies nose gorse, or just stand. Sunlight flickers across the windscreen as we drive to town for our session. I'm not sure what to expect. I'm not sure what I'm going to say. Now and again, I place my left hand in the warmth of Amy's lap, still holding the steering wheel in my right. After parking the car, we walk a narrow lane to a thatched cottage. Amy rings a bell, and a moment later the black door opens to a woman smiling.

She leads us through into her living room, which feels stuffy. The low ceiling, with its black painted beams, feels more like a lid. Amy and I nervously take our place besides one another on a small, leather couch. I'm in a T-shirt and shorts so whenever I move the skin on my forearms and behind my knees sticks to the seat. I'm not sure what to expect, how this will all unfold. Where on earth do I start? I hold Amy's hand as she sits down in front of us. I have already explained our reasons for being here over an email, albeit briefly, and I expect her to know what we might be going through.

What do you want out of these sessions? she begins.

Her questions put me out to sea.

I swim for an answer, clear my throat, my body a little shaky, *Well, as I said in the e-mail, our daughter died only a few weeks ago and we really need help.*

I'm so sorry to hear this. Boy or girl?

Well, if you had read my e-mail properly you would know we had, have, a girl. Her name is Elowen.

Oh yes, of course, I'm so sorry. It's been so hectic lately. She looks embarrassed, and struggles to say *Elowen* correctly.

In the pause that follows, any hope I have drops away.

What are you both doing at the moment, to fill the time, keep busy, as it were? Any hobbies? How about you, Amy, any hobbies?

My heart sinks further. I want to leave.

We've being going on a walk every day, together, and gardening with family. We've even got a pottery class booked but I'm not sure I'm up to it.

Do you bake? directing her question to Amy.

Not really, I'm a terrible cook, she replies, a little embarrassed that she has never been interested in cooking. She looks away. Her cheeks are flushed. I shift, getting more and more restless.

Anyone can bake, the counsellor continues. *It's really important to find a hobby. You must have more hobbies, Amy?*

Before Amy even answers I stand up.

I came here to talk about a dead daughter. Is this a joke? Are you even a counsellor?

My outburst leaves her stunned, and I feel ashamed.

We walk over to the door.

I'm sorry, but this isn't going to work. I'm sorry.

Before she responds, I pay her for the session, £80, and we leave the house. I feel better for being out in the open air, where I can breathe. We drive home, feeling defeated.

At home, Amy and I drift from each other. She does some gardening with her mum; I try to carve a piece of wood, picking up the axe that I last held when I carved Elowen's little spoon, bowl and plate. I then dig a hole, and keep on digging. I sit by the hole when it's finished. I go to light a fire but cannot. I am restless, hyper-vigilant. I am also exhausted.

Days later, we get a call from the Firgrove Centre – the charity-based bereavement centre that the midwives recommended, which had, at first, no space to see us. They are now able to take us on, and we make our appointment. It takes over 90 minutes for me to tell half of the story – I don't know why I went first; Amy's turn will be at the next session. From the Monday morning until a few hours before the birth, I choke on every word. I gasp for breath through every scene. Tears come, and silence, during which I hold my head in my hands. The touch of Amy's hand on my knee throughout feels like an anchor. Every detail of the days of Elowen's birth flood my mind, yet finding the words to describe what happened, out loud, and in order, seems impossible. Each image is an insurmountable hurdle, each feeling an eruption too violent to withstand.

Before we leave, the counsellor asks me to close my eyes and name everything in the room: the colour of the walls and carpet, the number of chairs, ornaments. I remember none of it. When I open my eyes I see the room again, the details. The temporary amnesia has gone. I name what I see. I feel calm, but drained.

Grief is a landscape without signposts, the counsellor says. *And I am here to guide you through it as best as I can. Before you leave, is there anything you would like to say to Elowen?*

The question hits me hard.

I miss you Elowen, I miss you so much, I say, the tears returning.
Amy is crying too, saying *I love you Elowen, I love you and miss you.*

Once a week every week we go to our session. Just as with our daily walks together, out on the heath, the hours spent together watching TV in the evenings with the teddy bear between us, they provide some kind of focus, markers in the quicksand of time. Despite this, we work hard to get up in the morning, see out yet another day. Making sense of a landscape without signposts feels impossible. Our hearts are daunted, broken. *Trust your gut*, the counsellor says at one of our sessions, which means I must trust the thing that hurts the most.

It's also about simply functioning. We live six hours at a time. Mostly less. We rise together, wash together, eat together, walk with Daisy and Dilly on the heath together, walking the same loop that takes us past the oak tree, and out in the wide land of heather. It is on one of these walks that brings us towards a mother and father with a pram, strolling in a beam of sunlight. We double back, walk the other way.

Being outside is the only way we can build some kind of structure in our days, being close to Amy. And that solace continues when I enter the Firgrove Centre, climb the narrow stairs to a room that has become a part of our life, and talk about our daughter for at least an hour. But I am still unable to tell our story out loud. When will that day come? I feel good that Amy and I are here together. It makes sense. I want to hear Amy's every word, to be here for her, for us. I cannot see how being here alone would help. It's not something we have talked about. Sharing this space with Amy feels as natural as going on one of our walks. Amy says she feels the same.

Back home, after counselling, we often head upstairs to stand or sit in Elowen's room. We go through her clothes. The dungarees. The little yellow dress has become an exclamation of absence. I run my hands across the newly painted wall. We do not part with anything. Then we go for our walks, or garden. I cannot bear to read. The pages of words do nothing for me.

Weeks go by like this. Another session comes, defining the looser routine of walking, talking, not talking, eating, washing, breathing, crying, yearning. I ignore texts from friends. I find online groups of bereaved dads, then discard them because I can never find a story that is exactly like ours. I have started to dream of Elowen, the first since she was born, both dreams as monumental and overpowering as the birth itself. Sleep is no longer a refuge from the day's sorrows.

In my first dream, I am standing at the edge of a forest at night. Behind me is our cottage. The light of Elowen's nursery is on. A shadow comes and goes across the window, Amy perhaps. I climb over the fence and make my way down into the forest. The fir trees stand tall. The scent of spruce resin is strong. It's not like a dream at all. The moss is thick underfoot. Sticks snap as I walk, and I can hear the call of an owl. A narrow track, pocked and rutted by deer, is slightly less dark than the surroundings: the darkest shade of silver. Following the track, looping between the trees, running straight into small clearings of bracken and birch, a very small light becomes visible in the distance. A single, very low star, perhaps the illuminated eye of an animal or a torch pointing my way – it draws me towards itself until, suddenly, as if I have opened my eyes, I am in a bright clearing. The darkness surrounds me, but at a distance. There is no sun in the sky, but it is as bright as a summer's day. I can see a figure, sat in the centre of the clearing on the stump of a large fallen tree. As I near, the figure becomes clearer and clearer until, from about two metres away, I see that it is a beautiful girl. Her knees are drawn up to her chest, her bare arms wrapped around them, her hands clasped together. Her face, turned towards me, is pale and radiant like the colour of moonlight. Her eyes are large and blue. Her hair, long and auburn red, flows down in loose spirals over both her shoulders. She is wearing a dress elaborately sewn with patterns like roots and branches. Her bare feet, half extending over the edge of a tree stump, are as pale and radiant as her hands and face. The stirring, almost unsettling, familiarity of her is mesmerising. I am sure that I have met her before, her image lingering on the edge of memory. Then she speaks, smiling first.

Hi Dad, I'm so happy you found me. She smiles again which lights up my heart. *I am so happy I have found you too, Elowen.*

I wake crying.

Amy holds me in the dark.

The dream was not a dream. Every part of me feels it as real.

I met Elowen, Amy, I met her.

Recounting my dream to our counsellor is almost as hard as retelling the story of Elowen's birth. I burst into tears when I describe the dream to her, and what Elowen said. The effort of putting the images of the dream into words, then voicing those words, leaves me exhausted.

Two nights after this, I have a second dream: Amy and I are making our way down a steep and rambling staircase in the dark. It's made from blocks of uneven stone and extends for at least fifty metres down to a beach. I look back up the staircase and realise that it leads down to the beach at Bedruthan Steps in North Cornwall. When Amy stands beside me I see that she's younger, and is wearing the same light-blue raincoat she wore when we first visited Bedruthan in the early years of our relationship, entranced by the beach and each other, holding and kissing in the sands, exploring the huge rocks and caves, running from the incoming tide, wading to safety at the steps. In the dream, though, the tide is far out and the Atlantic is a distant and constant roar, except when a full moon appears and the white lines of breaking waves lights up. As we walk by moonlight, I spot what looks like a seal floating in the calm between two waves. Amy urges me towards it, to get a closer look, and I see that it is a child, face down, naked. I know it is Elowen. I don't need to see her. She is buoyed on a rising swell that grows and grows into a wave that crests, stalls, her small body always visible in the moonlight and stationary for a breathless moment at the very top of the wave, before it curls and falls and she disappears. I do not know where she's gone. The waves are too strong to wade against, swimming is useless. I am pushed, thrown back on the cold, wet sand. Amy is so very far away, diminishing to a silhouette, then gone. Clouds swallow the moon. There is only darkness and the boom of the Atlantic.

I keep returning to the counsellor's words, *Grief is a landscape without signposts.* I can see that landscape now, dark grey, like a granite escarpment, with no horizon and an ashen sky. And when I look out across this landscape, I always hope to see Elowen – a small yellow light, a flame on a cliff-edge, guiding me. My lips remember when they kissed the bridge of her nose.

But I do not *remember* Elowen. She is here, surely. Because I am here. Because Amy is here.

Out on the heath, I begin to run. I did not plan to run. I do not have energy for it. But this evening, I break into a run, to a distance between me and home that walking can't do quickly enough. Walking makes me feel heavy, as if my bones have become stones that I can barely lift.

Trust your gut, and it's saying *RUN*.

I put one foot in front of the other, and soon I am running. I do not care that it will soon be night. I do not care how long or how far I go. I do not care because time has no meaning.

I run for as long as I can, pushing my body onward with a rage that reaches further inside. I run even though I am almost sick, well out of sight of home, well beyond Elowen's Oak. All I want is to run. It is the first thing I've wanted since we left the hospital – a desire for my heart to pump, for the blood to flow, for my lungs to work. I run as the sun disappears in cloud and, miles out on the open heath, the rain starts lashing. The wind rises, too. I see wild ponies crossing the forest tracks, deer-shapes gliding over the heather. I am relieved that night is drawing in. I am running towards the darkness. I am running to be erased. I hate the sun, the day, as much as I hate life. I am done with the things that once made me feel alive. I crave the dark now. My senses feel shrunken. During the day, things are just too much, pressing for attention, for energy I do not have. The pressure to talk, the pressure to grieve, the pressure to feel, the pressure to live. The pressure to feel pain. Everything just bearing down. Every sound too loud. Every sigh too bright. And this overwhelming sense of being followed.

Beyond the last trees, the heath becomes more like a moor, rising gently to a plateau. I stop on a hillock that rises above the heath. My body cools, my breathing slows. Out here, I have found a kind of winter, somehow. A place where summer has been rejected. A season of rain and night. All around me, the heather hisses in the wind and rain. I close my eyes and sit on the wet ground. I hold my breath, and listen to the drumming of my heart. Senses gone, the outer world shut out, the pressure relents. Until the inner world fills, suddenly, with images, sounds, smells. The panicked look on the midwife's face as she tried to find Elowen's heartbeat, Amy's hands over her eyes when she heard that her daughter has died, the cremation we didn't attend but which is relayed to me now as vividly as if I were there. The smell of the room where we left her.

I stand again, and run, run down the hill, over the plateau, I run until my legs can no longer take me, and I am falling in the mud and through hollows deep with rainwater.

Grief is a landscape without signposts.

I stand and walk the last stretch towards home.

When our cottage comes into view, I feel the pressure build up around me again, the knife thrust. I step through the door into a dark and silent house and see that it's past midnight. I have been running for at least four hours.

Standing in the hallway, dripping wet, I see Amy before me holding Elowen, and smiling, pleased that she had finally fed and gone to sleep without fuss. I reach out to them both, and reach right through their ghosts till my hand hits the wall.

We rely on counselling. It is the point around which everything swings.

Weeks of trying to say her story, our story. I bring her endless questions, I bring her my anger, my hate.

Why have I spent so much of my life trying to love the trees, the rocks, the rivers, when that world let my daughter die? Why have I always tried to be a good person? Why did this happen to me? I am angry. I am angry at always being a good person, too, angry at my niceness, angry at the person that was forced to hold his dead daughter because I bet if I was someone else it wouldn't have happened. How did she die? Did she suffer? Where is she? What am I now? Who am I without my daughter?

Our counsellor, sitting close, looks straight at us and tells us to shut our eyes and breathe.

America

Clouds move, seas roll on.
Day, night, pencil their pictures,
erase, pencil, erase again.
How to curb the sickness
that comes from all this motion?
Lie down, they say, *lie down.*
What arrives is already lost.
That's it, there there.
Breathe.

The anticipation of seeing a baby on the plane fills me and Amy with such fear that I almost turn around. To see a live baby in the arms of its parents would floor us. We know it's something, one day, we will have to face, but not now, please not now.

I peer down the plane, scanning near and far seats. No baby, no baby girl. The wave of relief that comes over me nudges me forward, bringing me face to face with a stewardess, her pale open hand, each finger extended with long nails painted with a violet varnish, waiting for my boarding pass. I'm also nervous about the long flight to San Francisco because I don't want to be left with my thoughts. Once the flight is underway, however, I sink into a routine of napping, watching repeats of funny programmes and films – *Alan Partridge, Curb Your Enthusiasm, Extras*, anything with Will Ferrell in it – and gazing ahead thinking of the morning she died, the birth. I push close against Amy for comfort, for safety.

The idea that somehow the big, wild landscapes of America might absorb the magnitude of the pain cropped up during our weekly conversations with our counsellor. Is it too much to say that nature, which I have loved and leaned on most of my life, *killed* Elowen? My anger needs something to blame. But I feel that if I turn away from nature, what else can I turn towards? My identity, what has made me, unravels under the force of this truth. And I am left with less than whatever I thought I was. Nature doesn't care, and yet I loaded my care into it. That's why I need to stay close to Amy – I mustn't be a fugitive from *us*, to believe in what is *human*, what cares and what really does love, and the strength of that.

Trusting my gut in this instance meant surrendering to my urge to flee, to get away. To run away, and somehow – I don't know – feel like we have some control over our life. I am also, I think, searching for a sense of continuity. Because travel played a cherished part in our relationship, we are going to revisit some of the places Amy and I went almost a decade ago. And it is this prospect that seems like a refuge from the upheaval and devastation, as if the past is a place of solace where we can glean strength or stability. Maybe. I don't know. I'm not convinced. Right now, everything is a door into the dark.

It seems like it's anyone guess, at times, what will become of us, and yet, we are here. I want this trip to be a devotion to us. We are holding on, just like the days Amy and I lay on our bed together, clinging to one another through the blurred days between finding out Elowen's heart had stopped and the birth. We feel sad for leaving the teddy bear behind. But our parents will go to the house to check on it, and to make sure nothing has happened to Elowen's room or any of her things.

We are travelling with Amy's sister, Hannah, who stays in San Francisco for a few days while Amy and I drive ahead towards Monterey. The highway is wide and fast. Trucks quake the tarmac. We catch glimpses of the Pacific through mountainous dunes and flashes of big, clean cars that shimmer north and south. We reach Carmel in the dark, staying at The Lamplighter Inn. Nine years ago, days after our university graduation, we drove Highway 1 from LA to San Francisco, staying in Monterey. We had always wanted to return. Big Sur, Point Lobos, Garrapata, Carmel – the sense of nostalgia in these names grows more powerful with each piece of clothing we remove from the suitcases and splay open on the hotel bed. I put my clothes away in the cream-white drawers as a sense that we are *actually* here comes home. It is a little less like a dream.

We walk beyond the last street lights of downtown Carmel, into almost total darkness, tripping over pine roots that have ruptured the sidewalk, scuffing through mounds of sand deposited by west winds and bare feet running up from the beach. We hold onto each other's arms and make our way towards the sound of the ocean. The white lines of cresting waves are visible in the moonless night, moving with urgency towards the beach, bending in bows across the sand, sucking back into the Pacific. What wind there is comes from the exhalations of falling, crashing waves. The air is warm, deep, and heavy. As I stand with Amy, arm in arm, on the beach at night, I think of whales and other mysterious bodies haunting the Monterey Canyon – a submarine trench deep enough to rival the Grand Canyon.

During our trip years ago, we only stopped briefly in Carmel. I ran the length of the beach and threw myself into the cold water to invigorate myself after the long drive. A wave struck and almost dislocated my shoulder. No one else was swimming. The few people that were on the beach watched on as I clambered out of the chaos of water, clutching my arm as though I had been chomped by a shark.

It's too late to swim tonight, and we're both jet-lagged. We leave the beach at around midnight and walk back up towards the streetlights. At 4 a.m., I wake to the sound of Amy screaming and the stark lights of the hospital, to the wan face of the doctor that told us our baby had died. I hold her so tightly.

Breakfast at the inn is spent dodging conversation and the inevitable question: *do you have kids?*' As Amy and I have shut ourselves away leading up to the trip, the sheer number of people in the dining room – not even a crowd – is overwhelming, so we duck out before the awkward rituals of familiarisation between strangers get underway, grabbing food on the go as we saunter down the main street towards the beach. The cold mist that was lingering is gone by noon, giving way to a cloudless sky of such blue intensity that memories of our trip together when we were young are jogged into the present.

Outside a shop of eccentric sculptures and woodcarvings, I hold Amy and tell her that I love her. Dogs run to and fro along the beach, the white sand rising in plumes from the digging and running paws. We talk of Daisy and Dilly. We sit down amid a hoard of Dalmatian puppies trying to be kept under control by an owner hidden in a tangle of dog leads, who eventually fights free with a grin of exasperated celebration.

South of Carmel, at Point Lobos, we are gifted the sight of two humpback whales rearing up through turbulent waters, yawning with an eerie drone of hunger, then submerging with throats engorged.

Pelicans drift, wings oddly kinked, veering around the headland, following the whales back towards Carmel. We race around the headland, finding a vantage point through contorted cypress trees, watching the whales breaching in sleek, titanic curves, then sinking deep like an entire world gone underwater.

Sea otters laze in a calm cove made even more still by the structures of kelp beneath the water. These forests have the sea's surface as their sky, and their floating, undulating canopies appear to be such a singular mass that I picture myself walking out across the sea.

In the late afternoon we drive south, first to Big Sur, then doubling back in time for sunset on Bixby Bridge. Driving north along that stretch of coast brings back the memory of seeing Big Sur for the first time. I remember the terrifying moment we discovered we were driving on the wrong side of the road after leaving the redwood forests; we missed a head-on collision by the width of a tyre; the long and loud truck horn blasted through us, the eyes of the driver were furious under his red cap.

At the bridge, ravens barrel-roll around and through its great arch, which is structured almost like an eye. Waves pound the black rocks below, rock plastered with guano and dotted with dozing seals and their faint yells that echo up the cliff. Pelicans disappear into the fiery crimson sun, then reappear on the other side, slower, more in shadow. Other couples and families are watching the sunset from the lay-by, some with selfie-sticks held aloft like signs at a demonstration, cameras flashing, laughter spreading. Occasionally, more cars pull off Highway 1, skidding to a stop as though in emergency. The click and thud of car doors opening and closing irritates me − selfishly, I want the scene to ourselves. I want it to be Amy and me only, standing here ten years ago, eyes bright with bliss, looking out towards our future.

Back north from Bixby Bridge, towards Carmel, on Garrapata Beach, we watch a dozing pelican get swallowed by a wave, and then spewed up further down the shore. It wriggles to its feet, collects its wings, and lifts out beyond the waves. It's the first time I have ever seen a bird caught off guard by the sea and almost get drowned.

Down from a creek bordered by profusions of Californian lilies and long, undulating grasses, we write Elowen's name in the sand. We sit together for a while besides her name. It's cold in the shadow of the cliff. We put our hands on her name and say it, *Elowen*.

At the far end of Garrapata Beach we sit down under a makeshift shelter of driftwood. The crashing waves are too loud to talk over, the sight of the Pacific too enthralling to turn away from. A father and his young daughter walk hand in hand, bending now and again to pick up abalone shells. Amy looks at me. I want them to disappear.

Fallen waves sweep quickly across the sand, leaving long kelp strands glistening translucent and tinted green in the sun. I whip a strand that is at least six metres long into the air. Amy grabs one too, and soon we are laughing, chasing one another across the beach, close to the sea.

I hate leaving Elowen's name alone in the sand, but our need to keep moving is strong. In an effort to rescue more happiness from the past, we visit Santa Cruz fairground on our way north to San Francisco. But the bright colours are garish. The crowds are too raucous, queuing in long, snaking lines for rides and screaming from an overhead blur of red steel and tracks. All of it is completely at odds with the feelings of peace we were carrying with us from Big Sur.

After picking Hannah up from a hotel in downtown San Francisco we head north across the Golden Gate Bridge, where I again catch sight of our younger selves leaning over the rail and gazing down together at the currents ripping and curling around the base of the red towers, giving the impression that the bridge is a ship moving across the Bay. I see younger Amy and Will hold hands and take a hundred photos.

We stop and have breakfast at Sausalito, but have to walk out of the café because a father and mother are cradling a baby only a few months old, the age Elowen would have been.

At Point Reyes, now a few hours from San Francisco, we stop again. I'm not sure if it's nature or the lack of people and noise, but I'm grateful for the space. We watched elephant seals burp and gurgle from a cove lapped by waves heaving with seaweed and kelp. A coyote jumps out from high, yellow grasses, pausing in the road, looking straight at us, then leaping into cover on the other side.

I drive the winding road to the far tip of Point Reyes. A strong west wind whacks the car, the land narrowing, the sight of the Pacific opening out left and right as a lighthouse rises into view ahead. We park the car and walk beneath a tunnel of cypress trees scrolled into shape by past winds. To the north there's a wild and desolate beach, grey waters and dark islands on a horizon. Though it's summer, it feels wintry. A peregrine shoots up overhead, and keeps on shooting up too high to see.

We drive on from Point Reyes to Guerneville in the dark, headlights illuminating tall and short roadside eyes, riven trunks of mammoth-sized trees, dark gulfs where the road suddenly disappears and reappears around a sharp bend in the coast road, oncoming headlights flashing strong against the darkness beyond. The sky is starless, the moon waning.

The damp in our B&B room is overpowering. At breakfast the owner assembles all the guests – a total of six – round a single table, making for an intimate meal. For Amy and me, this is intimidating. A pregnant woman reveals her bump as she rises from her chair and walks over to the coffee machine. When she sits back down, the woman beside her immediately reels off questions about her pregnancy. The mum is shy, private, unwilling to answer. But the other lady keeps on badgering for answers, her enthusiasm to know the ins and outs of the mum's pregnancy become more rude and invasive. Amy begins to cry at the table. Hannah puts her arm round her, as do I. We stand up and leave, the creaking of the chairs disturbing the silence of the other guests, and bringing an end to the women's interrogations.

Amy and I go outside beneath the redwood trees. Hannah bravely goes back in and explains to the owner why we left.

Being on the road again is a relief, lifting the pressure of having to meet people and answer their questions. The fragrance of the forest, the sight of rivers, the wind rushing across our heads, the dilapidated shops and swinging signs, the sky for its blue enormity. We pass a man at a crossroads holding a peach in his hand like he's only just discovered it. Tall eucalyptus trees line the road along golden hills. All this movement is soothing, rushing through, not dwelling, not letting the pain get me, outrunning it. I am glad Amy insisted on a convertible.

At Jenner, sixty miles or so north of San Francisco, we stop for lunch. A tall blonde man behind the café counter is so high on weed that as he slowly pours the coffee, he misses the cup. His eyes, bloodshot, gently open in a very delayed reaction to what he's done. Coffee pools on the chipboard floor. He raises his eyebrows, laughs, tries again.

Outside, wind from off the Pacific beats the river's edges into frothy waves that splutter over the bank. A lone snorkeller kicks upriver against the current. As we walk towards the car, a bald eagle passes overhead, its rippling shadow slow to follow on the dry ground. We watch it scale the hilltops above Jenner and the wide Russian River.

In Mendocino, two large dogs playing outside a bar remind Amy and me of Daisy and Dilly back home, so we stop and watch. Hannah is already in the bar, ordering drinks. We join her and sit down in a row at the bar flanked by two men in forestry shirts, sawdust on their forearms, the thick smell of oil and petrol ladening the air around them. We immediately strike up conversation, our heads turning left and right. The man next to me, from Fort Bragg, originally from Seattle, is looking for a fresh start after a break-up. We discover a shared love for *Twin Peaks*, and the other films of David Lynch. Amy goes over to the jukebox, and 'Surfin' Bird' by the Trash Men soon bursts into the room after a run of Black Sabbath. Amy, Hannah and I dance, or try to. Others in the bar, strangers, watch on, raising Sierra Nevada beers to their mouths in unison.

Later that night at the B&B in Mendocino, Amy and I confess our guilt over enjoying ourselves at the bar. We forgot Elowen. The shame of having laughed hurts. The shame of not being at home, the shame of leaving her behind.

In the morning, we keep talking of how we shouldn't be here at all, how we should be back home with her, caring for our baby. Our trip shouldn't have happened.

Where is our daughter?

Where do you think she is?

I don't know, I don't... Amy says, unable to finish the sentence, turning her head away, looking out to sea.

A hawk is scanning the clifftops in purposeful swoops and glides.

Leaving B&B and the cliffs behind, we walk the quiet streets and along the timber boardwalks roughened by feet and bleached by salt. The sun is flecked with a sudden appearance of cirrus clouds. I look at our reflections in the shop windows, seeing ourselves pass.

On our way out of Mendocino, bound for the Redwood National Park, I buy a small slab of redwood from a saw mill. The grain is dark and wide-spaced, the bark rim soft like a fur.

As we drive out of town, I think that I would like to return to Mendocino one day. The sea, its forested hills.

At Trinidad, we write Elowen's name into the dark gold sand, her name facing south towards a coastline of spruce and redwood and steep bluffs of dull silver rock.

The road to the redwoods hugs the banks of the swerving Eel River which bears north from Mendocino county for 196 miles before piling into the Pacific Ocean south of Humboldt Bay. Mist doesn't rise from the milky blue waters but moves along with the current, cold and slow. The car roof is down. The air is earthen, dense and wet. Fog clings to ghostly green branches that appear, now and again, above us. As we veer away from the river, the road straightens towards the Avenue of the Giants through the Redwoods State Park. Vast trunks, dark brown and riven with torn and fibrous bark, bulge out into the road. We crane our necks upwards as the car slows. Dawn was hours ago but the night still seems to hang in the shadows of the trees.

What would Elowen have thought? I say to Amy.

Amy, Hannah and I stand inside a redwood, a grotto with interior walls burnt black, scorched by fire and polished to a sheen. Looking up reveals a hollow tunnel, and above that the solid mass of the tree extending to over 300 feet. I imagine a wild fire whipping around us.

I take photos of Amy and Hannah wrapping their arms around the Founders Tree, its 40-foot girth dwarfing their hugs. Hannah takes photos of Amy and me. We walk alongside the Dyerville Giant, reputed to have been 362 feet high before crashing down in 1991, a fall so heavy it was measured on a nearby seismograph. Beginning at its roots, which splay out in a labyrinthine crown of twists and turns, we trail our hands along its sides as we walk in its shadow, following a timeline spanning 2,000 years from root to top.

In the afternoon, we drive north to Prairie Creek State Park, a site of coastal redwoods still within the state park. Here, we follow a creek that glistens beneath huge ferns drooping under their weight of green, the creek purling and deepening through forest that grows more dense as we follow the trail.

Stepping up onto a bank and into another fire-hollowed tree, Amy and I take a few moments of silence to absorb the surroundings, to think of Elowen. Hannah walks on, knowing we need some time to ourselves. Amy sits down on a natural step of soil and root beneath me. I rest my hands on her shoulders, and pull her gently back into my lap. I lower my face into her hair. I hold her close.

We love you, Elowen, we say, together, addressing the giant redwoods.

As we leave the redwoods behind, I am *trying* hard to be uplifted by these surroundings. But I want to close my eyes and see no more. I am tired of appreciating the world. I want to keep moving, to settle on nothing. And the urge to keep fleeing, look quickly at things, get in the car and go, gives me a sense of control. But how long can you outrun yourself?

We slow the car as an elk makes her way out of the forest. She crosses the road, stopping briefly to gaze around, her nose wet and gleaming, tall ears flickering. Engine off, we watch her pass. Her soaking fur steams in the sun. She makes her way down a steep ditch on the other side of the road, and walks into the forest.

As we drive out of the redwoods, the sky opening out before us, we can still hear the shrill bugle call of the elk, which seems to emanate from the trees themselves.

*

On the way to Willow Creek, we are delayed for hours at Trinity Highway as a wildfire leaps across the mountain pass. It moves like lightning, conducted by the retaining timbers stacked either side of a bridge above the Trinity River. A home and cabin are in cinders, charred and smoking among the burning aspen and spruce trees. The whole mountainside is black. The fire is still raging and running elsewhere. Helicopters swarm with buckets, in a chase to douse the flames. So much fire in my mind. The redwoods need fire to grow. I can't stop myself thinking of Elowen.

From Willow Creek it's on to Reno for a night, via Lassen National Park, then onto Salina, taking Highway 50, the 'Loneliest Road in America', stretching from West Sacramento, California, to Ocean City, Maryland, on the east coast.

At Lassen, we walk the perimeter of a blue, alpine lake, through aspen groves, and forests of spruce and Douglas fir. We then take the higher road to King's Hat Creek, and sit quietly in the evening by a meadow of golds and green, sliced in half by a clear stream that reflects the snow-capped peak of Lassen Volcano.

Hannah stays for a moment beside the meadow, while Amy and I walk the road's edge and look out across the hundreds of square miles of the caribou wilderness, evergreen forests tumbling away to a snowy horizon as far we can see. A cold wind blows against us, snow clouds gather over a darkening sky, and a weak sun smoulders in the west.

Snow falls as we descend the steep road. The roof is down so I sit up on the headrest and open out my arms, and the wind bites and the snow falls into the car as Amy drives down the mountain pass. The distant peak of Mount Shasta catches the last glow of the day, its snowy summit shimmering with patterns of silver, gold and red. I stay up and out in the cold wind.

It's almost noon when we enter what feels like the first stretch of loneliness on the Loneliest Road. The sun is hot and bright. My glasses are flung off my face by the wind, and we stop so I can search for them in the hot, dusty verge. A pick-up with a trailer loaded with timber rattles down the highway past me, almost losing control as the driver swerves and the trailer rides on two wheels until it rights itself, leaving a trail of parallel black stripes snaking this way on the shimmering tarmac. I find my glasses, lens down and scratched on an ochre coloured boulder.

Up over that shallow rising slope of land, the road becomes a straight, dark line extending as far as the eye can see into desert country. The car eats up the miles and the fuel as the road reels in under the bonnet and shoots out behind us.

I take the first driving shift, which brings us, via Fallon, towards Austin, Nevada, where the four lanes of the highway narrow to two. We have seen nothing but endless blue skies and desert climbing towards mountain ranges that rise up abruptly from the basins.

We stop up in the high desert. Nothing comes for miles around. Hannah and I lie down, star-shaped in the middle of the road. I close my eyes and can hear our breathing and feel my heart beating in my chest, moving up and down beneath the desert sky. A golden eagle flies beside us, only a few feet away, low to the ground, then sweeps away towards gathering storm clouds that are stacking up and up over distant mountains. The clouds seem to explode upwards, broad, deep and wide, becoming a singular mass of sky.

We keep going, crossing the Great Basin towards Utah, skimming across the surface of Nevada, the sun setting behind a range of mountains that form a wall on the far side of the basin. The peaks glow snow-pink. When we pull over to watch the desert darken, Amy walks away from me when I try to hold her hand, heading away from the road and into the expanse of rock and dust. I had said in the car how I hated the way she goes stony quiet when I know she's thinking about Elowen. I now desperately want to talk to her, but let her go alone for a while.

When I join her, we hold one another, unaware of the mountains turning into shadowy monoliths of crimson and pink. Amy's left shoulder is damp from my tears. My left shoulder is damp from hers. We walk back to the car together, and sit in the back while Hannah drives the last leg towards Salina.

A great shine of stars litters the moonless sky. Again, we pull over, right on the Utah border, and gaze up all together. I think of nothing but stars until I bring my head down and suddenly see Elowen in the Chapel of Rest, her skin greying around her eyes, and the thick, stuffy, fragrance of lit, rose-infused candles in the room, as many candles as there are stars above and around me. I am not in America any more, not in the desert, not on The Loneliest Road. I am there in that room. I lay her down in Amy's arms. The trace of her weight stays in my arms.

We drive on, over the border, into Utah. Dust kicks up from the tyres and spills into the night. I look back up at the stars now and again through the window, but am drawn more to the blackness between them. I would give anything to hold her again.

The following morning, when we stop at Moab, I argue with Amy in a shop. It leaves me completely drained. I think it was about Elowen, it must have been. Or about talking more to one another. I hate myself for it, and walk out of the shop to sit on a rock in the hotel car park, shielding my eyes from the sun.

Amy is resting on a large boulder inside Arches National Park. She falls to her knees, ashamed and embarrassed, having noticed that she has become incontinent. Her pelvic floor was weakened during the birth, and after laughing her way over higgledy-piggledy rocks, troughs and rises of loose stone and sand, she breaks down and blames herself for killing Elowen. Her words are hard to hear through tears. She draws breath. I hold her close but there are no words.

Later, when I am swimming in the pool at the hotel on the shores of the Colorado River, lightning sprawls across the sky. The canyon flashes silver and red. Staggered rages of thunder sound like intermittent rock fall. A group of people I had seen earlier in the hotel restaurant quickly vacate the jacuzzi, couples frantically throwing towels around one another, heading for the changing rooms. They look at me, afloat on the pool's surface. In front of me the canyon wall rises magisterially over the river. I close my eyes.

I am scared as the lighting flashes more often and the thunder gets nearer and nearer with each explosion, but I don't want to get out. The storm is thrilling. I draw a deep breath and sink down beneath the surface, into the blue and moving glow. Lightning flashes above.

A terrible ease blooms through me like a sedative. I could do it, now. I could drown. All I can hear is my pumping heart and the filter whirring and sifting in the far corner of the pool. Elowen comes into my mind. Her face, her closed eyes, her hands. Her existence suspended in the dark glow of my mind like a pale star. I put my arms across my chest and lay on the bottom of the pool. Then I think of Amy sat waiting for me on the cabin's veranda. I want to get back to her. I miss her. I suddenly need to breathe. I burst up through the surface, gasping. The lightning and thunder have moved direction, the desert air is revived. A lone osprey flies away from the canyon.

Back at the cabin Amy and I keep an eye out for the first stars that gather above the desert like lanterns held up by ranchers on horseback. We hold one another. I am still in my towel.

*

It's Hannah's final morning with us before we drive her to Salt Lake City, from where we'll continue with our trip to the southern desert of Zion. Amy and I haven't been alone for a while, not since Monterey, and even before that, back home, we were under the watchful care of family. Even without the support of a loving chaperone, I feel confident – and determined – that we'll be strong enough to be alone together, to look after one another, perhaps because I'm more aware of our fragility than ever.

Back at the room, after we pack the car, Amy and I stand beside the Colorado River. Amy is making a small, braided ring of grass as a gift for Elowen. When she's finished, she writes Elowen's name in a patch of sand, taking care over the shape of the letters and the way they join together, then places the green ring on the surface of the river. It spins and whirls away, but then gets snagged among other grasses. After retrieving it and tying it to a stick, I launch it further down river. As it travels out of sight, we say *We love you, Elowen*.

In the distance, straight ahead from the lodge entrance, stands Castleton Tower, a huge plinth of red rock, bright and raw in the sun, bleeding orange and pale crimson. Leaving it in this light morning, the road enters a deeper run of the canyon that is still dark and cold. The plan is to head east, then north to Salt Lake City.

We pass back through Moab, shining under the desert sun as we drive through it. Shop windows ripple like water, cars gleam. I look into the rear-view mirror at the sight of the Colorado River diminishing, then disappearing as we speed out of sight. I wonder where the grass ring is now.

The sign for Canyonlands says it's only 60 kilometres from here. At first, I wish we had more time to go there, but the need to keep moving dissolves this yearning, and we keep going. With the sun-roof down, I can look up at the blue of the desert sky. Hannah is driving, with Amy in the passenger seat. Now and again I lean forward to hold Amy's shoulder. I wonder what she's thinking. I dare not ask.

The silence is OK for a while, but becomes an enemy when my mind becomes filled with images and sounds, most of all that doctor's face and her lips moving, *I'm sorry but your baby has died*, then Amy clasping her head with her left hand.

The heat of the sun overwhelms me, as does the light, and the wind. I find it hard to catch my breath, really hard. We pull over. I have to get out. I don't even wait for Hannah to slide the seat forward as I rush and scramble up and out of the car and stray off the road, my breathing becoming more and more shallow until I'm forced to sit down. I put my head between my knees. Close my eyes. Darkness. No light is allowed in. No more light.

Amy kneels down beside me. Hannah does the same. They talk to me but I can't hear them. I can't even hear the roar of cars on the interstate.

When Amy's voice cuts through, I lift my head and look out across the desert. I stare. My breathing deepens and quietens. A lizard, lithe and bronze, stamped with patterns like the sole of a boot, disturbs the dust and leaves a trail no wider than my forefinger as it slithers away towards a signpost for Green River. I wonder how far the lizard will go.

Rising to my feet, I say that it must be the heat, being fair-headed and all. In the back seat, Amy sits with me. I swallow a Valium with a swig of water. We draw the roof back down, and I feel more at ease in the cool and the dark.

I am looking forward to finding our own rhythms again, rhythms of talk and touch that we haven't really shown while Hannah has been with us. We are so grateful for her love and support on the trip, and now she's on a flight, Amy feels guilty having left her sister to run our hostel after Elowen's passing – mostly admin, e-mails, helping with bookings. Hannah will step into that role again when she gets back, at least until we finish our trip, although Marc, who has been there since Cristen left, has been very understanding and assures us that he can handle things.

Now we have ten days ahead of us, during which we will spend time in Zion National Park, then revisit places we went to on our first trip to America together. We are getting used to being around people more, and the presence of crowds is not as overpowering. I am still terrified about seeing families with babies or young children. I cannot shake it. I just hope that these last days will continue the threads of connection between Amy and me, and between the present and past that are slowly being stitched.

When I glance across at Amy, or look at her sitting alone in the car from the window of the gas station, as I pay for fuel, I again wonder what she is thinking. I love her so much, and in fleeting moments like this, the love I feel eclipses the sorrow, the numbness. It's like we are twenty-one again.

*

Our tent is pitched on a terrace of rock and sand just outside Zion National Park, looking out towards the Kolob Plateau. Before we go to bed, we sit for a while on the small, timber deck. The sun is setting, and the distant cliffs, escarpments and ledges look like a pattern-work of wounds, dimly raw and red in the last of the light.

Amy wakes me in the morning, standing by the bed with the white sheets pulled back. The mattress is soaked through and stained with blood. The way her body is behaving – continued lactation, a weakened bladder, the discomfort of her ligaments and muscles, interior tears, the stretch marks she shows me every morning – is a constant reminder that she should have Elowen in her arms.

While she showers, I bundle up the sheets and take them down to the hut that is the campsite reception. I'm nervous about explaining what happened, but find the strength and words, going into full detail about our loss. The receptionists takes a step back, and immediately I regret explaining it. She then leans forwards, taking the sheets, and says *I'm so sorry, that's terrible.*

I could have lied, I could've said something else.

I stumble back up to the tent, my arms full of fresh, white bedding.

The shuttle bus takes us to the final stop, where only Amy and I, and a lone hiker get off. He steps off and determinedly walks further into the canyon, towards a pinch-point between cliffs and the dark bend from which the Virgin River flows. Above, the sky is a channel of radiant blue with jagged edges that are the very edges of the canyon walls, much like a sky-borne image of the river itself. The tops of the canyon walls are golden and bright, the Navajo sandstone flushed with a rich and ancient light. We are in shadow. It's cool and quiet, the shadow is a relief from the desert fluorescence. The river bubbles and runs wide and shallow through sandstone, flowing over gravel beds and courses through sparse crops of aspens. There is no wind. The coolness of the river can be felt in the air.

At a wide bend in the river, after more than two hours of following its course, we sit and write Elowen's name in the silvery silt of the bank. Water glugs on, and water weeps from the high walls opposite, dark stains from hidden springs. I hear voices. Voices breaking into laughter. I stand up to see a family coming our way. I see what must be a father with a newborn in a sling about his chest.

We have to go, we have to go, I say to Amy, with the same kind of alarm I would have if I had spotted a cougar stalking us down river, or Amy would have if she had seen a tarantula. Not so much a fear but a phobia. I am completely overtaken by it. So desperate am I that our escape from the dad with his baby becomes a kind of a hunt – he and his baby taking on the role of predator, we the prey. The whole escapade becomes so fraught with irrational fears that become laughter as Amy and I break into a light jog, putting in real distance between us and these predators. I feel ridiculous, but weirdly triumphant when we lose them entirely. I let my fears rest as we stop for a breather, but my nerves return as I start dragging stacks of deadwood and bundles of brush over the faint path we're on, covering our tracks, blocking the way entirely so that the family, if they even reach this far, will either have to turn around or cross the swift and deep river to get to the path on the other side. I still laugh at it, but the fear is real because seeing a newborn or a dad holding his child, puts me straight back in the hospital when Elowen was born, and I heard the tumble of what must have been her lifeless limbs falling, limply, onto the bed. Here, by the Virgin River, in this canyon, I am running for my life from a baby and her happy dad out on a hike.

The following days bring on further explorations of the canyon, taking shuttle buses to various points around the park, continually on the move. Our final day is spent on the outskirts of Zion, hiking a smaller canyon that cuts down from the Kolob Plateau. A small, emerald stream shimmers in the hot sun of noon. Aspens flutter and rasp in the warmth, their leaves announcing the turn into October with lemon-gold and apple-red. Beside the trail, there's a small log cabin, the timber rotten at the saddle notches, the door free of its hinges, balanced against the log-ends, where a sign reads *Mountain Lions have been spotted in this area recently.*

Up above the canyon, we walk far out into the hot, breezy air on a spur of land that juts out above the desert, a kind of flat fin of sandstone with views towards Zion, and further beyond to the Grand Canyon. Amy takes a photo of me standing at the very edge. Then a young American couple offer to take a photo of us both. We smile and squint into the light, sweat beading beneath the rim of my hat.

Beyond Las Vegas, the mountains of Nevada seem to float above the desert floor, their bases mirages of disappearance, shadowless and trembling, as if detached from the Earth. A high, barbed-wire fence lines the sides of the road for hundreds of miles, with military signs reading *No loitering, No photography, Trespassers will be prosecuted* situated on the fence at measured intervals. We are passing through the Nellis Air Force Range and the Nevada Test Site: the military and nuclear occupation of this vast landscape creates an eeriness of surveillance.

That evening, we take Route 95 to Beatty, so-called gateway to Death Valley National Park, where we spend one night in a run-down motel and learn that we're not that far from Yucca Mountain, currently identified by Congressional Law as America's storage facility for nuclear waste. Along the main street in town, burnt out pick-ups, clapped-out trucks, machinery, bundles of miscellaneous engine parts are strewn along the edges. There is hardly anyone around. I hear music from the open door of a shop. An old man is in the doorway of a boarded-up saloon, his back turned towards the road, standing there like an American cliché from a Spaghetti Western. But there is a lingering atmosphere here, of abandonment, which makes Beatty an interesting place, marooned in the Nevada desert, with sight-bending mountains and a mind-bending eeriness, along with its proximity to nuclear history and covert Governmental doings (with Area 51 lurking nearby). The desolation is appealing. The sand, the rock, the heaps of scrap-metal. If I could draw a picture of a place that says how I feel, I think Beatty, left alone at the edge of the great Death Valley, would be it, not the redwoods or the highways up and down the coasts of California. Swallowed in heat and sun and dry rock, ringed around by the dry Amorgasa river, there is a desolation here that is attractive to me. Its bleakness is beautiful, like the darkness that surrounds my dreams.

Once up in the morning, after getting supplies from a vending machine outside our room and refuelling the car, we take Route 374 to Death Valley National Park. It's the first night, since the Chapel of Rest, that I have forgone Valium before sleep. Mountains flicker far off. The road descends into a low-lying world of sweltering heat, dryer and more formidable even than the Great Basin that we drove through from Nevada into Utah. Death Valley is a cracked, white-hot plate stretched out as far as the eye can see.

Over ten years ago, on that first trip together straight out of university, in mid-August, coming into Death Valley the other way, from the Sierra Nevada mountains, our car broke down. A series of clunks, followed by the thick stench of burning rubber, the hiss of the engine, and steam billowing from the gap around the bonnet. The temperature read 129 degrees Fahrenheit on the car thermometer. Adjacent to our car, there was a signpost that read Furnace Creek, 22 kilometres. What water we had warmed instantly. The tarmac road was as hot as a stove-top. But by sheer luck, we managed to break down near the only emergency phone we had seen since entering. Amy sat in the scant shade of large boulder while I picked up the phone, the receiver too hot to press to my ear, and entered 911, tapping the numbers quickly so as not to burn my finger tip. After a few rings, a faraway voice answered. I explained our situation, then the line cut off to a crackling mixture of dial-tones and clicks.

Time passed slowly in a frazzled delirium between sitting together in the boulder's narrowing shade and standing to survey the swimming horizon, until, speeding across the open desert, sending huge volumes of dust and sand into the air, I spotted a black and white 4X4 that eventually skidded to a halt across the whole width of the narrow road in front of us. Out stepped a sheriff, boots clunking on tarmac, his face cool and calm beneath his broad-rimmed hat, his eyes concealed behind tinted sunglasses. He was even chewing on a toothpick, for goodness' sake. He brought out a gallon can of water, and threw it on the wheels of our car. Yanking the bonnet up, he tossed water onto the engine. The car fizzed and hissed. Then he suggested, in the least words possible, that one of us stay with the car while the other go with him to Furnace Creek.

Leaving Amy alone with our car, I sat up front with the sheriff. Between us was an array of firearms padlocked to a steel rack that spanned the width of the car while also acting as a screen between the front seats and the back. He didn't say a word until we pulled into a settlement of dwellings blistering beneath the sun. Incongruously, we passed a swimming pool, in the grounds of a hotel, where sunbathers cooked on barbecues around the edge of the blue water. Red bodies lying stomach and face up.

Crazy, the sheriff said, glancing at them. Then, pulling the vehicle up outside what looked like a rudimentary stone building, he got out.

I worried about Amy, waiting for me in the desert. But before any major anxiety got hold, the sheriff was back in the car, with gallon cans of water.

More of this and your car will be fine. I've seen it all before – tourists pushing on the brakes too hard as they come down the mountain pass.

He was right, of course. With further dousing of the wheels, the break pads cooled and the engine fired up, meaning we could speed on, with more caution, towards Parumph and Las Vegas.

Back in Death Valley now, years later, coming in from the other side, with the Sierra Nevada mountains our next destination further west, I keep an eye out for the Furnace Creek signpost and the telephone.

When the road descends to the lowest point in North America, namely Badwater Basin, the temperature rises and keeps on rising until we eventually reach Furnace Creek. The heat is like a billowing wind that hits when you get out of the car, flapping and grabbing at your body. The area is only half-familiar. I can't see a pool. The stone building where the sheriff got the supplies is gone. I wonder if my memories hold true. There's a new National Park Visitor Centre that claims centre stage. Beyond all this, beyond the coming and going of cars and people holding umbrellas as sun-screens, each person with a bottle of water held to their lips, the salt flats of Badwater Basin glimmer like a white sea.

As the road starts to gradually ascend out of Furnace Creek, a view of dunes opens out to the north, silken waves of silver-white sand rising and falling. Then I see the phone, and pull over. I approach it with a weird kind of reverence, lifting the receiver, letting my forefinger hover over the dial, 9-1-1, to meet the past.

Out of Death Valley, before we leave the desert behind, we pass a lone man pushing a trolley brimming with camping provisions along the side of the road, his hair and beard long, face, arms and legs tanned and burnt. Then just outside of Bishop, in Inyo County, 400 miles from Yosemite, we're pulled over by a sheriff for clocking 90 mph, and after a hefty fine and denying accusations of being drunk straight out of partying in Las Vegas, we drive on, reaching our hotel in the dark.

Snow falls across Tuolumne Meadows in Sierra Nevada, at 8,600 feet, inside the Yosemite National Park. The snow is blown in flocks that melt against the windows of the car. Up here, in the high Sierra, it's winter. The drastic change in geography and temperature from the heat and dryness of the Badwater Basin this morning is beguiling. I look around, mystified by the winter scene.

Lying on the hotel bed, after a quick dinner in the restaurant (ignoring families with babies, but not running away from them), then playing shuffleboard and table football (Amy always wins), I am excited to be back in Yosemite after that first trip a decade ago. I think of this place often, picturing the Merced River sparkling beneath the granite tower of El Capitan. Visiting Yosemite, like all the other stopping-places on this journey, is an attempt to create a new map that reconnects our present selves with the past, to remember or re-imagine a life without grief.

Coming here again feels like settling unfinished business, joining my eyes now to my eyes back then, seeing how I see things now. But also to make those memories come back to life, give them lasting allocation, resurgence, in the present. Can it really be done? Soon I fall asleep, curled against Amy, thinking of the granite, the trees, the waterfalls.

In the morning, on our way back up to Tuolumne Meadows, leaving the hotel shortly after breakfast, with peanut butter and jelly sandwiches packed into my rucksack, we pull over at Tenaya Lake. A chill wind skitters off the surface, bright waves break on a sandy shoreline. All around is a lofty stadium of absolute granite. The sky is the bluest of blues. The Lake is beautiful. Although I'm eager to get back to the high meadows, we linger here, walking among the fir and spruce trees that sigh in the wind.

The road climbs higher, the temperature drops, and at 8,619 feet we arrive at Tuolumne. Snow from yesterday evening clings to the grasses, and drips as the sun warms in the sky. The air is crisp and clear, the scent of high, fresh waters, and the pulse of rock. It's early October, and the small timber cabin that is the visitor centre is shut for the season. Soon the mountain pass will be impassable by snow which will not relent until spring, when the flowers break through, and ice loosens from the rivers.

I breathe and breathe again, picking up the same walking trail, the Soda Springs trail, that we hiked all those years ago, me wearing my Tuolumne Meadows T-shirt, newly bought from the visitor centre.

Are they gone forever, those two people, unhurt by trauma, unscathed by loss? What would I tell them now? I envy them. And I pity them for what's to come. I follow them, with a full nine years between us.

At Soda Springs, around which a small cabin is built, we watch mineral water burst and bubble up out of the earth, then spill and run into the surrounding grassland, painting a small wetland that branches out like an outstretched hand. I remember this place as clear as water. The memory and the water itself is a tonic.

On the banks of the Tuolumne River, we write Elowen into the grey sand. Amy takes a photo of her name. The sky darkens under high clouds. It was here, on a warmer and brighter day, that we once watched a line of wild horses cross the river. Chestnut, bay, white and black gleaming in the Sierra sun. Once across the river, bolting across the meadows, we could hear the thud of their drumming hooves long after they were gone.

At the hotel, we look back through our photos of the day and at old photos of when we first came to Yosemite, photos Amy had uploaded onto her phone before our trip. I can't believe how young we looked. Yosemite looks unchanged, of course. And there, towards the end of our photos, are Amy and I sat on the very same bank of the Tuolumne River. Now Elowen's name is up there at 9,000 feet, most likely being covered in snow.

Plunging 317 feet, crashing into the rocks below with a continuous thundering that is audible from way down in Yosemite Valley, Vernal Falls creates an enormous cloud of mist that envelops everything.

Along with others, I see how close I can get to the falls before the spray becomes intolerable. The roar is deafening, the rocks are as slick as black ice under foot. I am drenched by the spray. Amy stays back in the fine mist; her shape thins to a silhouette as I head further towards the falls. The sound, the utter rawness of it, speeds through me with a vehicular power. It's invigorating. Last time I was here, I managed to get very close to the main body of the falls. Not this time. The waterfall seems so much bigger than me.

Picking my way back carefully through the maze of rock, I find Amy talking to a man who, breathless, is explaining that he's looking for his phone. He dropped it somewhere in the rocks. Amy tells him to keep looking, *You'll find it*. Later, climbing up the steep switchbacks that are cut into the side of an almost vertical wall of granite, the man runs past us again, telling us he's found his phone, and that he really appreciated Amy's positive attitude. He yells, *whoop! whoop!* and punches the air.

Rather then heading all the way up to Nevada Falls where, on our first trip, I swam in an emerald pool just shy of the edge where the falls sprint over and down a cliff, we take the trail through tall stands of Douglas fir and pine. We cross a timber bridge where another man drops his phone into rapids while taking a picture – he just laughs and walks on. On a natural platform of rock and roots, with views up towards the silver thread of Nevada Falls and down into Yosemite Valley, where the Merced River glitters beneath the sun, we rest for a while. This is where Amy and I once held one another for what seemed like hours in a warm pool, gazing towards El Capitan. As natural as taking a breath, Amy writes Elowen into the earth. I kneel down with her and we put our hands on her name.

Instead of driving back to the hotel, I try to reach Glacier Point before sunset. From there, the whole of the central Yosemite Valley can be seen. But, as the mountain pass twists and turns higher and higher, the bends getting sharper, I am forced to slow. Recent wildfires have burnt the forest to a cindered skeleton. Black and shrivelled trees, shorn of every leaf, stand bare, barer than a winter scene. Thick smoke brings deep haze to the air, making the early evening seem very dark. Now and again, fires flicker, licks of red-orange flame on the forest floor, riding up trees, or whirling in eddies around the scorched trunks. We slow down entirely to wonder at a tree made hollow by flames that still writhe within it, swirling up and out of the mangled thing. Thick smoke, grey and yellowish, puts a dim blanket over everything until the road finally brings us out high enough to leave the smoke behind.

It's dark when we reach Glacier Point. We missed the sunset. But in its place, a full moon shines on the smokey land. Trees burnt black are made more ghostly by moonlight. Yosemite, the Sierra Nevada, glows. The granite landscape is dream-like. There is an elemental hush

Bright dots, like stars, prickle the face of El Capitan. They are climbers, head torches moving slowly up the granite wall. In the quiet of night, we can hear the tinkle and clink of climbing gear, the swish of rope, and the conversations between climbers. Amy and I watch them for a while, the shimmying points of light, some faster than others, some coming to rest entirely, until we grow tired.

We drive back to the hotel – too late now for dinner. Tomorrow, we have to leave early for our final night in San Francisco. We spend the rest of the evening watching You Tube videos of climbers making their daring ascents of El Capitan.

As we open the heavy door and step through, the Saloon is unchanged. Even though it's not yet noon, there are figures at the bar, hunched over their beers. It's dark and hazy. We sit down in the very same booth, facing one another. Amy has the view of the karaoke stage.

Do you remember that first night here when we listened to that man sing 'Achy Breaky Heart,' the same guy who filled our car with petrol on our way here?'

Amy laughs. I love to see her laugh. Her face lights up. Her smile, her eyes. Such tenderness. The memories make us happy. We reach out across the table and hold hands until the waitress arrives.

Back outside, we walk down the road to where we stayed, the Groveland Inn. Even at $28 per night, it was punishing to our daily budget back then. We had to forgo lunches, walking at high altitude with meagre scraps. But the swimming and the scent of pines and the touch of rock on hand and underfoot, the heat of sun and the air itself sustained us. I saw how the Sierra was enough sustenance for John Muir, when he went out for days and nights with nothing but bread. Some places feed you, your body gets what it needs.

I hadn't even thought of going home until today, but it's time to head west to San Francisco, leaving the mountains behind, and the freedom that has come from moving on every day. Soon we'll be back to weekly counselling, and our cottage without our daughter. Her empty room. Her things. Us without her.

The emptiness that opens out in front of me is bigger and wilder than any landscape we have seen. Our daughter is dead, and I do not know what that means.

Skyscrapers appear, the shine of a big city. Its busyness and noise tightens around my airways.

We spend our last night at the end of Pier 34, watching the ocean move between the city and Alcatraz, the hills of Marin County and the Golden Gate Bridge. We talk of sharks and watch sea lions honk, wrestle and loll on the pontoon they've completely taken over.

We are back where we started.

Winter

My breath strays across the moon,
or the breath of one close by, who,
when I turn, is gone.
You did not breathe outside
so it can't be you.
Dew turns to frost where I stand.
Unwell owls fall away into darkness.
Everything is catching.

Now we are home, we're faced with the repetitiveness of parenting ourselves. Walking, washing, eating, talking, crawling together through this landscape without signposts. And just as we're getting somewhere, navigating the wilds of our loss, Elowen's absence hits us hard. What's built, whatever semblance of one's self is reshaped, becomes a ruin. We are pulled down. Any threads of confidence that I've sewn between myself and the world (the world I once loved, of trees and sky and water and life) are torn. So it starts again. The hating, of nature, of self. I keep close to Amy. As long as we have one another, everything is going to be OK. I still believe that.

Often I catch Amy standing alone in Elowen's room, her back to the door, holding a piece of her clothing. I go in, quietly, and stand beside her, then we both sit down on the floor, shoulder to shoulder, head resting upon head, trying to string together sentences.

As our counselling sessions have so powerfully shown over the months, we are having to start over again, *together*. Treading water together is far better than drowning. At times, we do drift apart. But we are finding one another now. I try to read books, but the only thing I am able to read are actual stories of parents like us.

I realise now that in the old life, before Elowen, I valued myself as an individual. A lone wolf. This has gone, and I hope it's gone for good. Now, who I am is whom I am with. If my joy in being amongst living things returns, then it will only return to the me that is now *us*. We are a family. I am not *me*, not *I*. These feelings began to grow as soon as I found out I was going to be a dad, and I am grateful they have remained.

★

Leaves fall, clouds gather. It's getting cold. Family visits happen, but not with the same intensity. Mum brings us food, as does Amy's Mum and Hannah. We feel everyone's love and support and it helps a great deal. Friends reach out far less. I drop contact, too, simply because I don't care what they have to say. Though family are always on standby, and their visits are very much needed and wanted, we are more on our own now. And America becomes a dream, blending with the past that can never be recovered. Although, I do think something has stayed. Images mostly, of empty roads, the cascading roar of Vernal Falls, a telephone at Furnace Creek. Amy and I chasing one another in the bright sun on Garrapata Beach, our shared awe at the breaching of the whales. Writing Elowen's name along the banks of the high Tuolumne river. These things really did happen, didn't they?

Do you think you will ever want to try again?
We asked this question together on one of our walks, and left the answer as *no*. But the questions keep coming out of me.
She's still here, Amy replies.
I don't know, I'm sorry.
We don't even know what happened to her, she continues. *There might be something wrong with me. I hate my body. I'm the worst mum.*
Amy looks away. Then looks up at me again, *I think we should wait for the post-mortem results first.*
Sorry, I don't know why I said it. It's Elowen we wanted. It's Elowen we want. Why would we want another baby? What happens if it's a baby girl? I'll think it's Elowen.
What will happen to us if we have another child that dies?
We both fall quiet.
But what would happen if our child lives?
To make another child, Elowen's brother or sister, is that really in us?
I think of the last time we made love. It was in Kefalonia and Amy was heavily pregnant with Elowen. I kept thinking I would crush her. We laughed about it, and just held one another instead. And before that, the night she was conceived, when I had a cold and we had been trying for a while, and it had become almost like a chore. Now, the

thought of being close to those feelings again, physically, makes me uncomfortable. But I want to be close to Amy, as close as possible.

If we have another child, will this be a betrayal of Elowen? I want to give her enough space and time, and I do not want anything to overshadow her, not even my sorrow. But is that even possible? To think of her without the pain?

I just want to be normal, a normal parent.

Trust your gut, the counsellor said. *Trust your gut. Knowing you and Amy now, I think you will do what is right for you both.*

We tell our story now in the sessions, something I once found impossible. Saying these things now, out loud, giving them voice, frees me up. It's like stepping into a clearing where I can breathe. Until the forest closes again, growing over. Sometimes, I fall into the trap of thinking, guessing the rhythms of this grief. But how stupid, how arrogant. It gets me when *it* wants. I'm at its mercy. The only way out of these riptides is to go with it, which is terrifying.

Lately, the counsellor has been ending every session with, *What would you like to say to Elowen?* And each time it takes a while to get our words past our tears. All I can say is *I love you, Elowen, I miss you.*

Today, I feel strong enough to rescue the part of me that used to be comfortable alone, walking, running or climbing, out in the woods, on shorelines and mountain tops. I want to try at least, test the waters.

I drive out to the Dorset coast with Daisy and Dilly while Amy stays at home with her mum and sister. I want to go on a long walk, just as I used to before Elowen passed. Running is different – it feels like fleeing. And the walks I do now with Amy, most often to Elowen's Oak, to stand or sit there, or pick at the wax left by our candles on the morning of Elowen's funeral.

The hardest bit is driving alone, with little distraction, because it always stirs up deeply uncomfortable thoughts, making evident how vulnerable I am in times of stillness. I do not want these thoughts in my mind today. I want a day off, a day out. I fight the thoughts away, telling them out loud in the car to leave me in peace.

I grip the steering wheel and scream until my throat is hoarse.

I am determined to prove to myself that I can cope on my own. The faces of Daisy and Dilly in the rear view mirror bring some comfort. I cannot bear music or the radio so make do by driving in silence to the Studland Ferry, where I dock, get out of the car, and stand on deck as I used to as a child with my dad holding me. I think of all the trips Amy and I have taken here to walk Shell Bay, from our first date when we were seventeen and set out in mid-November to walk the Purbeck Hills, the north wind bringing flurries of coastal snows that turned our faces blue. We have always returned here. The sea runs up against the side of the ferry which rumbles and groans on great chains to the other side. Gulls pass overhead, the sea churns. Ahead, the sands of Shell Bay stretch to Old Harry Rocks under a darkening, January sky.

Leaving the car at Worth Matravers and walking out towards St Aldhelm's Chapel, Daisy and Dilly run ahead urgently sniffing the high banks above the path. It doesn't take long for the pain and sorrow that I thought had subsided at the ferry to come back, at first quietly, brooding at the edges, then with a surge of darkness. I thought I had it under control. I try walking it out, picking up pace towards the sea, watching my feet beat the dusty track. But this doesn't work. Instead, each step pushes me to the furthest edge of my ability to cope.

I stand on the grassy cliff. The horizon is dark, rain lingers between here and the horizon as blue-black sheets of braided vapour. Where is there to go? I feel a great weight nudging at me, prodding with a cold sharp finger between the shoulder blades, pushing me towards the edge. I look down. There is no one else around. The sea is dark and still. Small waves break on the rocks below, spilling through blowholes, then sliding back like fading voices of all the things said to me that have broken my heart.

You've got to move on. You've got to have another baby.

Be a man, toughen up.

Oh well, you can always have another one.

Dangling my right foot over the cliff edge, I see myself down on the rocks, face down, my rucksack slung to one side, legs crushed beneath me, the waves lapping against my body.

I could so easily jump, shift body weight to the other foot and fall.

A simple movement, under my power, something only I can control. And I could let it all go, right now.

How can I ever address all the hurtful things said?

I am not strong enough to confront anything anymore, not with words or actions. I breathe and look out at the January sea.

Why can't they see that Elowen is here?

Do they not see that being a man is being a man in grief? And that being a man in grief is no different to being a man in love? Being a man does not mean denying this love for my child. Her life was short, in other peoples' eyes, and yet she is eternal to me. I am who I am because of that love. I shall not change that because of what others think I ought to be. My sorrow might embarrass them, or give them a sense of uncomfortable shame. But I will always stand with, and for, my daughter.

If I jump, there will be one less person in the world to say her name. One less voice to make the sound, *Elowen*.

I think of Amy, her face, her eyes.

She is so much a part of me, and I her.

I step away. I step right away into the grass, well away from the edge. It is a relief. The rush to keep my daughter alive takes hold, and I care about nothing else except the love I have for her. I may not be who I was before. I am changed, and that person is ruined. But in my love for Elowen, I am a man and her dad. Life has split vividly into before and after, and I want to live for my daughter, for Amy.

I walk on. I walk down the coast and sit among the rocks and watch the waves run and fall and roll out to sea, staring out for hours as the sky brightens, despite the passing veils and tendrils of rain.

Every now and again I glance up at the cliff I almost jumped off. Yet here I am, unhurt. Breathing, living. But full of anger, too, at the things I said to myself. But I must not try to understand them anymore. It doesn't matter. I simply want to be with Elowen, which is nothing other than being with pain, right at the searing heart of it.

The rain comes and goes. Gulls whip across the sky, and waves drive in, shattering like glass. A lone cormorant holds out its wings in a strung-up welcome. I cannot say that I feel better. All I can say is that I did not fall. If it is for Elowen that I stand, for Amy, then I will be OK. We have one another. All three of us. *I am going to be OK.* For now, one signpost at a time, we are making our own way across this strange, precarious landscape.

On the drive back home, taking the swerving road from Corfe to Studland, a black cat darts across the road. Its body hits the wheel. I get out and lean down to find the animal still beneath the car. I crawl under, and come out with its body warm in my arms. Its long black tail hangs over my forearm. Its eyes are glistening. I go from farm to farm carrying the cat in my arms. At the doors of a barn, a man in overalls steps out.

I'm so sorry, I say, *is this your cat? He ran under the my car. It all happened so fast.*

Just put him down there, the man replies, pointing at the tall grass by the barn. I lay the cat down, carefully, and put my hand on the fur. *I am sorry*, I whisper.

I walk back to my car with its engine still running. Before driving away, I turn to look but the cat is hidden from view by the grasses.

At Hope Cottage, we practice ceremonies, unplanned, on the spur of the pain. I walk in the woods at night. I take Elowen's photo to her oak tree – daily, nightly. Rituals, routines. I run in the rain with my head down, head torch on, washing the tracks, filling the streams. I say her name out loud when I run. *Elowen. Elowen. Elowen.* Stamping her name into the night and the wet earth. We take out her clothes, her yellow dress, fold them with care, and put them away. Then take them out again. We hold her teddy bear and cup her ashes. I cry her name, and laugh in her oak, and hold onto Amy through the nights when I can think of nothing but the birth, and that doctor mouthing *I'm sorry but your baby has died,* and feel the heat of the flames around the little coffin.

Amy and I hold one another at night. We kiss more, kiss through tears, and this closeness grows when we leave our home behind and drive out with Daisy and Dilly to central Sweden for Christmas. The three-day drive takes us, eventually, north of Mora, where we stay in a remote cabin in the snowy woods. I have always wanted Amy to see this part of Sweden in the snow. Again, following our gut, we are running away. As the sun rises so late and sets so early, the days are short but peaceful. We walk in the snow, look for moose. We toboggan down slopes, our laughter echoes through the forest. In the cabin, we watch movies and lie by the fire, drifting in and out of sleep. I feel at rest somehow, Amy too. We talk more openly of trying again for a child. The fear is still there. The fear of the child dying. The fear of us not loving him or her because the child is not Elowen. But there is also the hope of holding a living child, a child made by us.

We light a candle for Elowen on Christmas Eve, and place it between us on a bench outside in the snow where I have lit a fire. We sit in warmth and stare at the flames, talk, drink tea, eat chocolate. A towering silver birch tree, dripping with thick lichens and mosses, is illuminated by the fire. I look at Amy in the orange light of the fire, and feel a love that is almost overwhelming.

The drive back home is long, through sleet then rain, and any sense of rest is left completely behind in the forest, with another Amy and Will, when we get a call from the hospital. It's Amy's mobile that rings, and we are told that the cause of death is largely inconclusive. There were three kinks in the cord, and the placenta was aging perhaps too quickly. But inconclusive, nonetheless. Cot-death of the womb, we are later told. Six months of waiting. Six months of forcing it to the back of our minds. Six months of wondering, *were we to blame*? And now there is no reason why she died. Nothing we can pin our pain to.

*

When we get back to Hope Cottage, we make the decision to put our business on the market, sell the hostel and move on. We simply have no energy for it. We are through. We have no plan with what do next, though. All we know is that this phase of our working life has to come to an end, and it feels empowering to make such a bold change.

It does not feel like a risk. It feels absolutely right. Our time away from it, time to work on our grief and our relationship, has thrown what matters into perspective. Some things are clearer now. We know, at least, what we do not need. The final decision is surprisingly easy.

We need to be in Snowdonia to sort out the lists of tedious loose ends, but it does give us the chance to say goodbye, and to return to some of our favourite walks in the mountains, going over those early days when we started out, so young, too young, to run what turned out to be unmanageable. It took over. And now, with Elowen not here, we need to simplify our lives. There will never be a fresh start, but there can be another direction.

Staff leave, rooms are emptied, cleaned. Snow falls. Snowdonia turns white. We walk around Lynnau Mymbr, thinking back to our first days here – we were only twenty-four. Our older feet tread the snow now, and where other people will see two sets of feet, I see three.

When the final day of the sale comes, we leave the keys under the mat in front of the blue door with views up to Moel Siabod. We turn the brass handle for the last time, which I first turned when I came to stay here at sixteen. As we get into the car, the snow continues to fall at a slow diagonal across the hostel, across what is visible of Clogwyn Mawr. The thought that Snowdonia will be out of our lives suddenly hits us. We stall, dither, and instead of driving east towards home, we drive west, heading for Nant Gwynant, our old refuge, so we can walk just one more time.

Before we descend into the valley, we take the mountain road to Pen-Y-Pass. We stop the car, get out, put on crampons and pick out our ice-axes from the boot of the car, treading the ever-thickening snow up the Miner's Path. Tears come into Amy's eyes as we walk, glistening in the snowy light.

Elowen, she says, *Elowen*.

The dogs tear past, kicking up a cloud-burst of snow that is blown away by a blade of chill wind. Up high in the snow, traipsing with crampons up into the white, I suddenly become breathless. I need to sit in the snow and look hard at my boots. Amy catches up and leans down towards me.

I can't do this, I say with my eyes fixed on my boots. *I feel so weak. I can't believe she's not here. I can't believe she's dead.*

It feel so wrong to have to leave these mountains because Elowen died. This place has been our base, our home, for most of our relationship. It makes me angry that we are leaving. I feel lost. These mountains are a home. They are a part of me.

She's ruined our life, I say. *It would've been better if we had never tried for a child. I was happy before her, I was OK.*

Amy puts her arm around me. The dogs run in, poking their noses up into mine. For the first time that I can remember, I put off going to the summit. I don't want to climb among the rocks and ice and snow that have always made me me feel so alive. Instead, we head back down to seek out the trees and rivers of Nant Gwynant.

We decide to put off going home to the New Forest, and find a place to stay in order to extend our time here. A cottage named Celyn. We book it out for the next three days. It's bright white and set back into the belly of the mountain above the Glaslyn River, with views straight across to Elowen's Pines, the four, tall evergreens on a platform of rock. From Celyn, the pines seem to jut further out into the valley the longer I look at them. I remember that warm day in spring when Amy, Elowen and I walked up to them, and sat there listening to the wind, where we christened them Elowen's Pines.

Our first night in Celyn, I sleep well and unaided by Valium. Instead, the sound of the Glaslyn River rushing over stone and the wind through the trees lulls me to sleep. There is something about this place. Being here, the anxiety over selling the hostel has faded. The hurtful things I said, about Elowen, are left up the Miner's Path. The grief itself is still here, like the winter, because it is part of my love for our daughter. But I feel like I'm in good hands here, at Celyn. It's the same feeling I had when we first stepped into the counsellor's room and told our story. The same feeling I have always had falling into Amy's arms at the end of another day.

I leave Amy to sleep as I stoke up the fire and sit with a cup of tea in its warmth beside Daisy and Dilly. The sense of age in these stone walls is palpable. The walls are granite, wet to the touch. The smell of damp is strong, like the interior of the mountain on which it is built. By mid-morning, I go in and wake Amy. She smiles at the view, at the light.

Why do things feel less hard, less immense, all of sudden?

Why do I feel that life isn't only about coping?

We have three days here, and the thought of our home in the New Forest brings a sense of dread. Hope Cottage has become a place of darkness. Even the teddy bear and the yellow dress. I shouldn't admit this, I mustn't. And yet it's true.

After breakfast we walk the Nantmor road which takes us up high towards the Moelwynion range. At its highest point we take a footpath over moorland into a deep forest of fir trees and oaks, which stand out as craggy, riven anomalies. There is a freakish warmth in the light, the sun rising overhead. Winter's fist releases, if only for today.

Down at Lyn Gwynant, where, a few years back, we were going to get married until changing the venue for Hope Cottage, we sit at the edge of the lake. I cup the cold, still water and wash my face. We sit for a while and throw stones for Dilly who is brave enough to swim, then walk on and rest on a bridge that spans the Glaslyn River. We lie side by side, with the sun on our faces.

When Amy and I sit up again, almost an hour has passed. We slept. I look around for the dogs and they're asleep too, in the grass, in the sun, by the river. I do not feel happy. That would be going too far. But I feel something other than the numbness and pain. Something has cleared. I have regained a feeling that I had on my first encounter with Snowdonia, when I was sixteen and climbed the small mountain, Clogwyn Mawr. It reminds me of why we wanted a life here, and why we can't just leave. We have deep attachments, from a decade ago when I ran up the mountains, following every stream and touching as many surfaces as I could, all the way through to naming Elowen's Pines. These attachments mean something, surely.

★

On our last day we drive out to the Llŷn Peninsula, to its farthest tip. The wind is so strong it knocks me to my feet. The dogs bark and run. They love it. They go mad in the wind, just like they did on the top of Clogwyn Mawr all those times. I hear us laughing at them, Amy's bright smile in the wind. And I can hardly believe it, and in a sense don't want to. I am so used to feeling pain that my body doesn't trust these bright emotions. I must be conditioned to feel pain and sorrow, not laughter. We have no right to laugh.

Bardsey Island rises into the light. I can't take my eyes away from it.

After walking, stumbling through punches of wind, around the headland, we drive down to Whistling Sands. We drink a thermos of hot chocolate in the car. As the windows steam up, Amy writes *Elowen* on the window with a heart drawn beneath her name. Out on the beach, the wind blows crisp and fierce. The winter sun is setting. Gulls fling up over waves that run, crest and roll in like scrolls of light. I face the sea, and the flying gulls and the wind and breathe in as hard as I can. I breathe as though I have finally come up for air, found a hole in an ice sheet under which I've been trapped. I recognise parts of a world, parts of me. The pieces are floating towards each other, their edges ragged and raw.

Days later, back home in the New Forest, my mind runs back to Nant Gwynant often, especially to Celyn. Amy and I walk out to Elowen's Oak every day. Sometimes, I run to it. I hold onto its great trunk and still see, below the lowest branches, the marks where we held her funeral ceremony. I look, look away, and look back again at where we lit the candles for our dear girl.

Since being back, we've talked more about trying again. We talk. We listen. We walk. The results of Elowen's post-mortem have left us disorientated, but they also have made Amy feel more confident in her body – Elowen's death was not her fault. I have tried to help alleviate the guilt Amy feels over Elowen's death, but that is all I can do. She has been desperate to blame herself, to hate herself, her body. She even labelled herself as the mum that killed her daughter, the mum of a dead baby.

Maybe if I had just gone into hospital on the Sunday morning, or the Saturday night? What if? What then? She might be here with us now if I had just gone to the hospital earlier, demanded to get her out early. Why didn't I hold her when she was born? I'm such a bad mother. I'm not meant to be a mum.

I hate it when she talks like this. I do all I can to console her, which is not with words but by listening and holding her close. Hindsight is cruel. We did the best we could do at the time. Didn't we? There is nothing we, or she, could have done. There were no signs. She just died. Her heart stopped. Her breathing stopped.

Did she suffer? What did she feel?

We walk. We talk. We listen. We are quiet together, too, and that is getting us through this. There will always be a sense of moving through it. Perhaps we should never expect to step out.

So we try again. I hold Amy to me and feel the warmth. We are prepared for anything now, abandoning ourselves to one another in the throes of grief and love.

*

Snow falls all day on the heath, into the forest, burying the road. A few cars trundle past, slide and skid. By midday the road is silent,. Abandoned cars line the roadside, sunken in ditches, slumped in deepening snow that keeps on falling, blowing in from the north. Out on the heath, the north wind is bitter, but the dogs love it, their whiskers bristling white. Daisy blends in with the snow. Dilly stands out, golden and pristine. They run and run, furrowing their noses into the snow, losing themselves in the blizzard and the deep, white heather.

It is a white-out. We cannot see home. The wind blows against our backs as Amy and I walk on, arm in arm or occasionally slightly apart, responding to the undulations of what is normally the path. I have never seen this landscape like this before. It's as wild as tundra. The heath is the barest and most open place we could be. Nor can I recall experiencing so much snow in this part of England. I think of the skylark that I saw here last week, fluttering up towards the sun, floating down to the warm ground. Where is it now?

Instead of walking to Elowen's Oak, which we can see, just about, in the distance, we walk out in the white open. Out here, I feel very close to Amy. It's the first time since our trip to Nant Gwynant, staying in Celyn, that I have felt able to simply enjoy, though uneasily, the present moment. There is still this vigilance in me, a hyper-sensitivity to what could go wrong, which can make simple tasks like crossing a road tiresome, as I stand looking left to right, left to right, and back again.

Yet the drive to feel normal has been building. In me, this idea of 'normal' means regaining something lost, and the thrust of it is spurring me on to go back to Sweden, to look for wolves. Hearing me talk about it, Amy is encouraging. She says she'll be OK at home for a few days with her Mum. I don't feel good about going, but there is still that nagging need just to do the things I have done before. To be Will, to look for wolves. Both of us feel a desperate need for the world to carry on *for us*, for Amy and me. Yet we also want the whole world to stop, to stop what it's doing and pay attention to our sorrow, because that means it is paying attention to Elowen. Living between these two movements has been exhausting. Now, however, we are learning to go with it. Trust our gut. And this means trusting in what we do not understand.

And yet, the day before I'm due go, out here in the deepening snow, the thought of leaving Amy and the dogs for Sweden overcomes me, unexpectedly, as a sense of dread. Seeing wolves doesn't matter anymore, not as much as it used to. The excitement is hardly there. It feels more like a deflated habit. I start to wonder if the trip was booked prematurely, and that I had been deceived by positivity, that short burst of confidence. Why go over old ground? What if I couldn't rejuvenate interests that have become inert? I tricked myself into believing I'm the same old Will.

What matters is being with Amy.

Over the months, we have drifted away and towards one another, in all manner of currents: riptides, tidal drag, submerged in the same dark sea, always at the mercy of the overpowering movement of grief, a force unto itself. Taking on lessons learnt from our counselling, we are giving grief its space, surrendering to it. The alternative – denial, blocking out – has always seemed impossible. There is no doubt that we have fought our way to this point.

I feel like we have found one another on the heath, with the same intensity as all those years ago when she first pulled me beneath the waves. I begin to hope that the flight to Sweden will be cancelled. This Will, the one I am now, does not care about tracking wolves.

Waking at 4 a.m., I check travel updates. My flight is still scheduled to depart: the only flight leaving for Stockholm that isn't cancelled. I am disappointed. My bag is already packed. I creep downstairs, where the dogs are in their beds, Daisy with one eye open, keeping track of me. I open the front door and am met by a three-foot wall of snow that has been banking up against the door all night. Beyond it, more snow still falling. Kicking away the wall, my boots crunch and sink as I trudge outside, grabbing a shovel on the way to clear snow from the front gate. The car chokes, then starts. I haul my rucksack in and roll out, stopping to get out and close the gate behind. The rumbling of the engine and the click of the latch as the gate is secured are extremely loud in the silence of the snowfall.

Amy comes to the front door, wrapped in her dressing gown, Daisy and Dilly's heads are either side of her knees. I have never felt so nervous about leaving home before. A sense of frailty comes over me, bringing tears to my eyes as I walk towards Amy. She tells me to stop being silly, to be safe, to drive slowly, and urges me to try and enjoy myself tracking wolves in a place I love. *It's something that made you happy.* Her words give me a little bout of courage.

More cars are abandoned on the roadside as I drive slowly, the tyres splashing through slush, the windscreen wipers at full throttle, lights on high-beam illuminating the white road ahead. The long drive to Heathrow brings on thoughts of Elowen. Driving alone still does this, setting my mind whirring over and over a flashing trail of haunting images. They are always waiting there, at the edge of vision, seething to overrun me. Her lifeless body in my arms. Her greying face towards the end of our visits in the Chapel of Rest. *I am sorry but your baby has died,* then Amy lying back on the hospital bed, her hands over face. The closing of the door, the final scent of roses.

My pulse quickens, I lose concentration of the road and almost swerve into a bank flanking the roadside, catching my breath in quick gasps as I realign, drive on. I put the radio on to drown out the images and sounds in my mind. I want to call Amy, and try to relax into the drive.

It's the first time I'll be going to spend an extended period of time (three days) away from Amy since losing Elowen, and I really do not feel strong enough to brave the world. Will there ever be a time when I can think of my daughter's face and feel the same warmth I did in the weeks before her birth? How has it come to this? My daughter has become a source of anguish. I feel so hollowed out. The world feels so different to me now. It's removed, or I am removed from it. My name is Will, but I am someone else now, not the person behind the name.

As I turn off for the airport, following signs for parking, the sun begins to show itself above a dim horizon. By the time I am out of the car and walking towards the terminal, the sky is grey and white, except for where the rising sun begins to glow faintly. Still the only flight for Stockholm leaving this morning, is my flight – and it's packed full. Snow begins to fall on the runway. I call Amy, waking her from sleep. It's so hard to say goodbye. I stall switching my phone off as the plane takes off.

I wake from a deep sleep to a vast patchwork of white and dark green stretching as far as the eye can see. Wind streams over the wing that tips and rides the cold air. The plane dips into blizzard, bouncing on the runway that is hidden from sight, as is the airport itself, except for red and orange lights blinking.

The cold wind and snow is refreshing as I walk down the stairs from the plane, crossing the quiet runway. A guide is there to meet me this time, so I don't have to journey north on my own. Another member of the group has arrived from Denmark, and we all shake hands before walking out to an old, white bus that I recognise from the year before. In the front seat, Marcus, a guide I recall from the last trip, is a comforting, familiar face. I climb into my seat, turning my head around to greet the other members of the group. Six in total.

I fall in and out of sleep on the long drive north, the roads becoming quieter and quieter, the ice getting thicker. High moose fences run along the edges of the road like borders operating one country from another. We will be staying at the same guest house as last year for the first night, and for the following two nights we will camp in the forest.

Arriving at the guest house shortly before nightfall, I see my myself here as I was a year ago. An expectant father free of grief, uplifted and in high spirits. The lake behind the guest house is only partially frozen, and the forested island within the centre of the lake is exactly as it was. So is the small wooden boat tethered to the same rope by the shore, a year older, its blue paint thinning, cracking, peeling along its sides and hull. I walk over to where the sheepdogs are kept, but they do not emerge from the red barn.

When I walk into the guest house, I know exactly where to place my boots and where to hang my jacket. The owner greets us. He remembers me immediately, saying he is glad that I've returned. I walk past the room where I stayed, and up the winding stairs to my room for the night, with the large bay window looking out over the side garden and beyond the fence to the darkening forest. There are two single beds. I wish Amy was here. I throw my bag on one, and lay down on the other, messaging her to say I've arrived safely.

There's a knock on the door and a mellow voice saying *dinner*. I head downstairs where the sight of the two guides and the rest of the group sat around the dining table, freely conversing, laughing, makes me retreat into myself. I say very little. I avoid eye contact, and am relieved when the food arrives because it means I can be distracted by eating. Then a lady in the group decides to methodically work her way around the table, asking us, one at a time, to tell her a little about ourselves, if we have a family, what we do for a living, whether we have children. Luckily, before she reaches me the guide interrupts and talks to us about the plan for the next few days. I'm sure, when it came to my turn, I would have said I had a daughter.

It is minus fifteen, at midnight as we carefully walk around the edge of the lake, in wolf territory. Tall fir trees, jacketed with snow, arch over where we walk in single file, stopping now and again to listen. It's so quiet I can hear my heartbeat, and the breathing of the guide who is much further off, a hooded silhouette. I am very tired from the journey but the anticipation of hearing the howl of a wolf enlivens me, as does the cold and the sparsity of the landscape. The sadness of leaving Amy has left me. With each slow and measured step into the crisp, dark snow, I feel OK, free of grief, sorrow, guilt. I have forgotten just how much I love this landscape, and that tingling hope of hearing, seeing wolves. That part of me hasn't been crushed. It's back, and I'm so relieved to be here. I savour it. I hold on tight. I hold on because I am clinging onto myself.

A wind, out of nowhere, skitters across the lake, whisking snow into the air that blows our way in showers. Almost half way around the lake, we stop. The guide gathers us round, talking softly about how it was only a few days ago he found fresh wolf tracks here, and saw the wolf itself looking straight at him from across the lake, half-concealed in the forested edge. The wolf could now be near, far away, or shot dead by a poacher. When the guide whispers about seeing the wolf, I hang on every word, enthralled by his description of the encounter. The tracks are somewhere beneath us, buried under snow, proof of a life frozen until spring. With the same enthusiasm as my last trip, I want to walk and walk through the night, through the forest, around lakes, through snow to find a trace of the wolf. But it's 2 a.m. We work our way back to the forest road, and clamber into the bus. It's very cold. I look forward to a hot shower and sleep.

The following morning I call Amy – we are spending the next two nights out in the deep forest in tents, so I may not have a phone signal to call her. She tells me that the snow is waiting for me back home, and that yesterday, after I left, she made a snowman that Daisy knocked to the ground.

After breakfast, we drive and walk to an area I have never been before. I try to see if I can recognise certain features of the landscape, but it is all new to me. I half-wonder if it is my memory that has been compromised by what has happened, so much so that I ask the guide to make sure. He assures me that I did not track wolves in these parts last year, which I'm relieved to hear.

On the way, the guide points out a remote building, a seasonal research centre, that is used by biologists to monitor wolf populations through examinations of scat in order to procure the wolf's DNA. All known wolves are logged into a system which is open to view by the government, who, rather than the biologists or guides who have the wolves' and the lands' best interest at heart, have the final say on the allowance of wolf numbers. The moose population is kept high for political reasons, in order to appease the hunters who perceive and believe that the wolf is a threat to the moose, which they also regard as their own property, and livelihood. In a country of over half a million moose and two hundred wolves (the number wildly fluctuates), the hunters' argument doesn't stack up. As with other countries across the globe where the wolf once flourished, there is an irrational hatred that runs strong and deep.

As the bus pulls away from the research centre, I wonder if there will ever be a time when humans, in our seemingly infinite capacities for inventiveness and intelligence, will be able to share the world with wolves, and with wildness.

The snow is soft and deep. I am warm, tracking a set of wolf tracks along the edge of an abandoned logging road. We are all absorbed in following the tracks, careful always to walk alongside them as though the tracks themselves are precious and alive. Yellow urine is bright on the snow, and dark scat is littered beside it. We stop and stare. A raven whooshes overhead, alighting in a tall spruce not far off. Then another raven appears in the glaring sky, taking its place on a tree neighbouring the first raven. The presence of ravens and the trace of wolves, quite fresh, could suggest a kill nearby. We press on, following the guide as he steps off the road and into deep forest.

Blood speckled on snow, a broken line of it, leads us to a clearing. A dead moose is lying on its side, opened out and torn. There is still flesh clinging to flensed bone. Blue tits and other small birds flutter in overhead branches, feeding on the flesh with the bigger birds and mammals. I can't help but imagine the scene of the moose being chased down into deep snow. The wolves hanging on, driving it down, feeding. I wander off a long away from the smell and the blood, looking for wolf tracks but instead come across the perfect print of raven wings frozen in the snow. I remove a glove and run my index finger along the risen lines of the wings, the shape of feathers. The detail is remarkable. I wonder if these prints belong to one of the ravens we had seen on the road.

Back at the moose, the guide suggests we camp nearby. As there is still quite a lot of the moose intact, there is a possibility the wolves will return, or at least some other animals. Carrying all our gear, we head further in the forest. I come across a small, plastic green tag and as I pick it up from the snowy ground, half a moose ear comes with it. Moose No. 102. The tag comes away easily from the brittle, frozen ear. I put the tag in the side pocket of my rucksack, along with the black toe of the moose that is nearby. The animal has been spread far.

By the campfire, I get talking with another member of the group. Talk moves on to the reasons we have come on the trip, with familiar replies: wolves, wildness, home-life. Between what he says, I'm always vigilant for the topic of children, family, which is bound to come up. As with the night before, around the dinner table, it is intimate conversation like this that I have avoided for months now.

I hardly listen to what the man says as I breathe deeply, trying to stay calm at the chance he asks me the wrong question. The fear overtakes everything, and I start gathering pine branches to stack up the fire with, in the hope that my actions or the growing flames distract him, bringing an end to our conversation. The flame spurts, ticks and rises.

Do you have any children? he asks.

Yes, well, not exactly. We had, have a girl. She died not long ago.

How old? he asks.

A few days before her due date.

He goes quiet, looks down, away from my eyes.

I never thought it would take such a colossal amount of energy to say it. And there is still this disturbing thought that when I say *when* she died, that this doesn't quite qualify her as a full person. That a baby, a baby who died before she was born, isn't as devastating as say, a walking, talking child. I feel as though it's not even worth telling him and that makes me feel hollow. But why? I feel ashamed but also know that there was, and still is, a whole life waiting for her, one that she will never grasp. And so there is that grief, too. My mind does all this, in a matter of seconds, until another voice comes through, a wiser voice that doesn't feel like mine, assuring me that a child is a child, and longevity is no measure for the impact that someone can make, no measure for the sanctity and beauty of what is brief but everlasting. She is a burst of the brightest and darkest colours that are woven through my heart. So I correct myself, and find belief in what I feel.

A sharp intake of cold air brings me out of myself.

He doesn't say anything in reply. He casts a wistful look, then says that he is tired. He stands up and walks from the fire, nodding at me as he goes off in the dark towards his tent.

After a camp-fire dinner, myself and another, more out of a need to keep warm, go in search of wolf tracks. The night is starless, windless. It's incredibly still. Our movements steal the silence, as if a window has shattered. The others in the group stay behind sitting by the fire which becomes smaller and smaller as we tread further into the forest, our head-torches illuminating the darkness ahead. I feel a sense of relief, being away from the others.

The stench of moose carcass hits us. We cover our noses and walk around it. The blood and bones shine in the light of our torches, as does the moose's dark, large eye. There are no new signs of wolves.

Back on the road we pick up a set of wolf tracks that lead up the road. They bring us to a closed barrier. We duck beneath it and follow the track along an abandoned forestry road. We walk and walk. I could walk all night. The tracks stay on the road, in the centre, printed in deep snow, an irresistible trail tacking this way and that, swerving and bending and running into the distance. I am so caught up in following the tracks, I leave the other person well behind, only just in range of my torch light. I switch off my light and listen for his approaching footsteps. My body is hot even though my face is freezing cold. I apologise for getting carried away.

At night in my tent, I cannot sleep. It's minus twenty-five degrees, and I'm wrapped in two sleeping bags. I close my eyes, bringing my head into the cocoon of the sleeping bags, but am finding it hard to catch my breath. I don't care about the wolves. I hate myself for coming out here far away from home, and am overwhelmed by a terror of images. I am desperate to throw off the sleeping bags and get out, but I know that it's too cold. I have to lie here with my panic.

I breathe. I count my breaths.

Not since Green River, during our America trip, have I been so overcome by sensory panic. My throat is tightening. There is nowhere I can go. I think, I breathe. I breathe and think. My mind clears, and I see the beach at Garrapata, Amy laughing in the sun, and the pelican being driven under the waves and spewed out fine on the sand. And the whales and dolphins. I feel Amy close to me. She is here now. Holding my hand. I can feel her warm and slender hand.

I can breathe again.

I will stay awake all night and listen for wolves.

Out on the frozen lake the following day, we find more wolf tracks, prints preserved like an ornament in the ice. I run my fingers over their form, the hollows of the pads, the impression of the paw. They were here.

After setting up for lunch at the end of a thin peninsular of rock and snowy heather, we listen. We all listen. The guide walks out far onto the frozen lake. And howls. A perfect wolf howl. Protracted, long. A call. Then we listen. The air is taught with anticipation, drawn tight and wired. I am brought to attention.

After a little time the guide trudges back and asks if one of us would like to howl and call out to the wolves. No one raises their hand. Then I do, feeling a little embarrassed by my uncharacteristic boldness.

I walk out onto the snow-covered ice, and feel the silence around me, pressing under and over me. I wait, as if to be invited. A howl comes, through me and out. It's not as perfected as the guide's, but I'm pleased to let go. The howl ends. Then we wait, listening for a reply. I howl again, but this time with more strength. And it is a howl that touches on something raw, and very familiar.

Great howl, Will, the guide says. *Sometimes they answer, sometimes they don't. But they're out there, somewhere.*

I stand back from the ice and sit on a lichen-covered rock beneath the pine trees, and look out into the white, expectant land. What faint wind there was, is gone. Despite the sense of freedom in howling to the wilderness, all I really want to do is get home to Amy.

The next day, as Marcus is driving us back to the airport, when we slip back into phone signal, Amy calls.

I'm pregnant, she says.

VI

Candles

Frost grows upon us because we are so still.
The world has passed.
Did you see it go?
The moon remains,
illuminates
every blood line in our bodies
bright silver and white.
We sparkle on clear nights,
fade when clouds linger.
Through all light changes
we stay stitched
together by frost.
We are miraculous.
Watch us gleam.
Fear is the polestar.
Our home is loss, winter.
We no longer doubt
the presence of darkness and ice.
Fire is where we falter.
Fire is far too much life.
The loss of the sun
has made the old cold
our new warmth.
Admire us, then –
two monuments made one
under great and silent pressure.

We busy ourselves at Hope Cottage. I build a workshop; Amy helps, or she gardens, paints. We remain close to one another on our walks to Elowen's Oak which is now budding green after a long winter. Our closeness is strengthened further by our commitment to weekly counselling sessions. And with the hostel now gone – a huge part of our lives – we have even more time to concentrate on one another.

Hard though it is to still be in the house where Elowen died – in the same bed where Amy lay still and shocked that Monday morning, which only seems like yesterday; to stand in the empty nursery that is a shell compared to what it should have been – the centre of horror has slightly moved. Our counsellor, during one session, says that the haunted look is beginning to leave our faces. I know what she means but cannot envisage it as others can. We are here, we are alive. We are making it through. But really, there is no ending. Everything about Elowen and us – me as her Dad, and Amy as her Mum – is still unfolding. I will always be in the midst of it, just as I am in the midst of myself in the unstoppable motion of things. Terms such as 'closure' and 'healing' seem ridiculous. How can anything ever be finished when all is change, all is movement? I love her and want her and need her, and that will not stop. Those worn-out ideas that grief comes in stages is rubbish. Like love – no, it *is* love – it lives, and living is an indefinable process, well beyond the range of language, too intimate for words to uncover.

We are existing, for now, through this new pregnancy one scan at a time. We have scans once a fortnight. We are worried about it being a girl. I am convinced our baby will die. There is nothing to temper the concern. In our counselling sessions, there are now more things to try to work through.

Will it be Elowen, if it is a girl?

Will I love this child as much as I love Elowen?
Will Elowen be forgotten?

I bring these questions to our counsellor as though they are riddles to be solved, not experiences to be lived through. At the end of one particular session, she draws two diagrams on separate pieces of paper. On the first, she draws a small circle, and around it a much larger circle. The larger circle is our grief. The smaller circle is us. And on the second piece of paper, she draws two circles, grief and us, but similar sizes, and the titles of the circles interchangeable.

It will keep changing, she says. *Sometimes one will be larger than the other, and vice versa.*

If I had been shown the second diagram during the months after Elowen's death, I would not have believed it. But now I know she is right. I think back to the pool in Utah and the cliff-edge in Dorset. Was that really me, wanting to end my life?

I am so proud of you both, she says. *I am in awe of how strong you both are as a couple*, she adds.

Amy and I look at one another with eyes that take us, in a wordless way, to those shared parts of ourselves that have never faltered or frayed since we fell into one another on that moonlit night, in the sea, all those years ago. I *am* proud of how we are getting through this. That there will be no end is still overwhelming, but not, at times, debilitating. The guilt of being a parent again, however, is crippling. I can hardly bring myself to acknowledge, let alone, love this new life growing in Amy. I do wish to hold our living child one day, but somehow this all feels too soon, too quick. And yet my parent-heart yearns.

What about Elowen, will I forget her?

Will she be pushed aside into the darkness, along with the pain that is my strongest connection to her?

I love Elowen, but has she made me happy?

Will our next child complete us, bring an end to sorrow?

Will we be OK if this child dies too?

I wonder, constantly, what our one-year-old daughter would be like now, and what she would be doing. What colour would her eyes be?

Will she forever be our daughter with the closed eyes, at perpetual rest in their nests of shadow and frost? The daughter with the cold hands. At night, I am woken by dreams. Her skin again, greying, right before my eyes.

Sometimes, in my hate, I wish Elowen had never been born.

More scans go by. The baby is growing well. And we have decided to find out the sex, to give ourselves time to prepare. I hope that it is a boy. I want Elowen to be her own forever. I even get her name tattooed into my wrist, scarring her name into my body. My body feels blessed by her name.

At one scan, we are told that the baby is a boy. We name him Eli. Eli Owen Searle. At 20 weeks, he is measuring big. He is more active than Elowen was. Amy says she can really feel his kicks and punches. Elowen was gentle in comparison. The obstetrician decides, with our consent, that an induction is the best way forward, but tells us that it may come to a C-section because he is being induced early. He will be delivered at thirty-seven weeks, which will make Eli's date of birth 10th October 2018.

With this plan, Amy feels like she has failed again, failed in not being able to give birth naturally. She talks to our counsellor about her jealousy of other mothers. But in the end, she says she just wants a living child in her arms. Each week, Amy and I bring these concerns and questions to the counsellor. We talk through them, always leaving with a sense that we can love two children, that our hearts, put together, are big enough. One child dead. One child, hopefully, alive.

But can the heart hold these together?

I wake every morning expecting death, as does Amy.

He's not moving, he's not moving.

A son. I have a son. A son.

It takes a while for me to touch Amy's belly, to acknowledge this other life growing in her womb. But I'm trying, really trying, to let my guard down. Tentatively, I talk to him. I sing. I am careful not to get carried away. I put a stop to any future dreams. We are not excited. We are wracked with concern.

After much searching, I find Eli his own oak tree. It's roughly a mile further on from Elowen's, and like Elowen's, it catches all the light, and stands out on its own under big skies and in big winds. I go there to connect with him, just as I do when I watch him move in his scans and listen to his heartbeat or feel his movements. Taking a little time out beneath Eli's Oak, I am often bowled over by the circumstances we have been thrown. I don't understand life. I am at pains to try make sense of it. Set up as puppets, subjected to this violent mystery of love and loss, joy and pain, the sense of feeling helpless is very real. We have thrown our arms up in the air with no energy left, but we have also thrown our arms around one another and endured, together. This is what I have to keep remembering: we are not alone, there is *us*.

I am held in the midst of a motion that will never stop, swinging between darkness and light. There is integration, not healing, not a closure. I am always open.

Lie down, lie down, a voice says.

*

In late May, we go back to Nant Gwynant. We rent Celyn again, glad to be away from Hope Cottage. I don't want to leave.

The regular scans have told us that Eli is well. We are relieved, but knowing this doesn't eliminate our fear that something could go wrong, at any moment. It would not be difficult to go mad with worry.

Often, in the afternoons, Amy and I lie down together at the foot of Celyn's steep garden, shoulder to shoulder, the sun warming our faces like an act of benevolence. Light has never felt so good, so needed.

I see the heron daily, taking charge of the river, surveying the water's flow and shine from the banks of ash and oak in full leaf. Leaving the river in the late afternoon, as mountain shadows spread across the valley floor, the heron heads northward towards Y Lliwedd. The bird seems as old as the mountains.

During the day, hundreds of swallows flit across the green fields of Hafod Y Llan, circling the sheep, flickering over the long waving grass that is brushed by a constant breeze coming into the valley from the west. The swallows nest in huge barns, the stone outbuildings, coming in and out in showers and flurries. House martins line up on the phone line that runs above the length of the road, and explode in all directions when cars or walkers occasionally pass.

Every morning, I sit outside the cottage and trace the shapes of the trees and mountains with my eyes as though my eyes possess a sense of touch, open and reaching. The warmth seems set to stay. Most mornings before breakfast, I leave the cottage and let Amy sleep. I walk down to the river with Daisy and Dilly. The river is too shallow to swim in, so instead I crouch in the cold, clear water, facing upstream, and then lower myself down to lie flat, face first on the river bed. The water rushes over me. I hold onto a rock and swing side-to-side like a fish or a weed. Daisy and Dilly watch me from the bank above, waiting for me to throw sticks or stones. I turn onto my back, spread my limbs, and look up at the blue of the sky until it is all that I see.

As I clamber out of the river and walk up the steep drive, dripping wet, and come in view of Celyn, a feeling of love comes over me. I have to stop halfway up the drive and look back at the mountains, the rich and vibrant greens that are particular to Nant Gwynant – a Nant Gwynant green. The sudden desire to take it all in, to be consumed by the place, comes as a welcome change: lightness instead of the heavy weight of grief that I have been carrying round. Something has helped lift that weight. I believe it is this place.

Despite Amy's fatigue and her understandable concern about over-exerting herself, we cannot resist the walk up to the blue pools and waterfalls of Afon Cwm Llan. Our relationship with the grief has changed. We are learning to embrace what makes us happy. We put ourselves first. Sometimes, we just need the distraction of the hills and the rivers to step away from the darkness, because at any moment grief does that, returns with another stabbing twist. By redirecting our energies into living rather than dying, life comes in. We have been gently tilling the loss, over and over until, something good, yet frail and fleeting, is starting to take root.

The first pool in a series which ladder up the mountainside, is as far as Amy wants to go today. These pools and waterfalls, cascading down from Cwm Llan, fed by streams that begin in Cwm Tregalan below the south ridge of Snowdon and the south-west face of Y Lliwedd, first caught my eye during our first year working at the hostel. While I was running up the Watkin Path, I was stopped in my tracks by the turquoise clarity and diamond shimmer of the pools below. From that moment, Amy and I would go to them on the rare days we had off and the sun was out. A place of escape, rejuvenation. I loved to swim in each of the pools, getting close to the waterfalls and diving down into the tumbling water.

The water is deep and clear. Round stones, dark blue, grey, glossy veins of copper, shimmer at the bottom. The pool is about twelve foot deep. I toe the water, always slow to submerge myself into the cold. Amy laughs, mocks me. Dilly barks, Daisy herds Dilly, lunging for each other's ankles. I retreat from the water's edge and make my way, barefooted, up the rough path above the other pools and waterfalls that burst over stone rims and pummel down smooth chutes. From this height, Amy and the dogs are out of sight. I can see Celyn, a white rectangle at the foot of the forested mountain, Coed Eryr. Beyond that, there are the wild plateaus of the Moelwynion mountain range, marked by the pinnacle of Cnicht at the far western end. I follow the distant Harlech shoreline with my eyes, until the coast merges into haze and sea further south towards Cardigan Bay.

Elowen's Pines, where we climbed this time last year, catch and hold the strengthening sunlight that enters the valley from the east. I watch the trees brighten. The surrounding mountains seem to move away to give the pines more space to shine, lending them a definite place in this valley, a landmark that I always bring my eyes to. In the quiet up here, I listen to Amy's laughter mingling with the sounds of the waterfalls, and her laughter becomes the water. I move to see Amy is in the pool with Dilly, who leaps in for a stick. I watch them play for a while before making my way back down to join them.

We hold onto each other, kicking and treading to stay afloat. Later on, the walk back down into the valley, we bump into our neighbour who tells us that once, years ago, she dived down into the very same pool and opened her eyes to the staring eye of a dead wild goat, one of the animals that haunt these hills.

Except for a few days that are humid and overcast, days broken by thunder and rain during which Amy and I swim in the deep bend in the river opposite Celyn, the warm weather stretches into June. We continue with our little adventures, acquainting ourselves with the Nant Gwynant. One day, I nudge off from the grassy bank and set sail across Llŷn Dinas, reclining in a black rubber ring and holding a beach parasol held aloft. Stop-and-go jounces of a warm, easterly wind propel me across the lake, towards the river. The mountains watch on. My escapade seems to fill the entire valley with delight. Sunlight gleams in stippled bands on the lake's dark surface. A heron passes silently overhead. A few drops of water fall from his outstretched feet. I laugh as the parasol snaps then crumples into a baggy, defunct piece of fabric – although I still use it in the shallows as a punt to hoist myself into the flow of the river, ducking under the bridge, catching the current.

After Elowen's passing, I came to think that the pleasure found in simple, makeshift adventures like these was gone. I was convinced that any enthusiasm for such fun was drained dry by the energy required in simply putting one foot in front of the other, by eating, sleeping, washing. Even now, despite the sense of hope brought on by the new pregnancy, I still believe that this kind of bliss is a lie, and that these hard-won tokens of elation will have to be paid back one day. Even the restorative energies of Nant Gwynant fail, on occasion, to shake this inner weight of defeat.

Amy chases my river-bound escapade from the track, walking eventually to the river bank, through a screen of silver birch and willow with Daisy and Dilly, who frantically bark at my progress as I roil around, getting wedged and unwedged between boulders over which the water froths and pours. Finally, I come to a scraping halt on a shallow bar of grey stones. I sit here for a while, in my rubber ring, face to the sun, immersed in the Glaslyn River. Beyond me looms Moel Hebog, and at its foot the village of Beddgelert. For a moment, I feel only the presence of the sun and water, the familiar laughter of Amy above the river's song, and the warm wind rushing, now and again, over me, and on ahead towards Moel Hebog which towers over the valley like a good dream. The heavy pain of losing Elowen, and the intense, overwhelming worry over the fate of our boy goes quiet. I feel as empty and as bright as the June sky.

Back at Celyn, sunburnt and tired, we are sitting on the sofa when we feel Eli's first kick. A thump around Amy's belly button. My hand is on top of Amy's hand. The kick brings about a jolt of panic, reminding us of Elowen's last kick.

Is he OK?

He kicks again, and again.

The next day at Morfa Bychan, a long stretch of beach along the Glaslyn Estuary, we walk out as far as we can go at low tide. We can see the Wicklow Mountains on the east coast of Ireland, a silhouette of knuckled land trembling through summer haze, as far south as Cardigan Bay, and out towards Bardsey Island. As we stand knee deep in shimmering clear sea, inland seems miles away, and so does the grief and anxiety, help and hospitals. We hold each other's hands, alone and far out from anyone. Purple, brown and yellow jellyfish bob by, bound for the shore on small waves that gather speed over the golden sand.

We know that Eli's life, like his sister's, could be snuffed out at any moment, that our own hopes as parents could be dimmed in an instant, and that our relationship could be hurled into another darkness. So we acknowledge him, yes, but this time we rein in our love, to protect ourselves. We do not want to fear anymore, even though our life is framed by it. We try to carry on as Amy and Will, filling our days with small spontaneous adventures outdoors. We continue to swim in rivers, climb hills, to embrace the life that we had lost faith in. We also take trips out west to the Llŷn Peninsula, spending full days at Porth Neigwl, walking along the bay towards the far end where R. S. Thomas, the poet, used to live. In places, when the mood strikes, we write messages in the sand to Elowen. I swim far out into the blue that is almost as blue as the pools of Afon Cwm Llan. At Morfa Bychan, we walked until it was deep enough to swim and I could no longer see the shoreline, where I held Amy, warm and happy, in our ring of light.

I do still wake in the night to images of her screaming and weeping as she gave birth to Elowen, and the silence that followed. I am getting better at letting these images run their course, and the question that usually follow. *Will Eli still be alive when morning comes around?* The sound of the river outside helps clear my mind before going back to sleep.

A drive south brings us to Aberdovey, where the estuary is a vivid expanse of sea and sand fringed by oak woods. When we had a full day off from our duties at the hostel, we would make trips down here and walk out along the lines of sand that stretch far out to sea, towards the sun. Once we fell asleep on a sand dune and woke up to find we were on a small island only just large enough for Amy and me. The sea completely surrounded us, glittering in the sun. We had to wade back to the shore in deepening water and strengthening currents.

I always loved the drive back north along the coast, taking the old timber bridge to Barmouth over the Mawddach Estuary, the rough timber boards clattering beneath the car. This time, there is no hostel to rush back to, no customers to welcome, no toilets to clean or beds to make. We park the car and walk to the centre of the bridge. Crowds of pale ochre reeds sway and seethe in the wind. Clouds gather above the mountains, their shadows cloaking and slowly sweeping across the hillside, undulating with the shapes of the hills. Beyond, the Irish Sea is golden blue, the horizon a dark bar. Gulls pass overhead in front of the sun, disappearing and reappearing. Amy and I step up to the rail, holding on as though we are on a ship setting sail. We seem to have all the time in the world to appreciate this moment.

*

Every table is candlelit in an otherwise dark restaurant. I pull out a chair for Amy and try to push her in under the table. She laughs at me straining to do so because she is thirty-seven weeks pregnant now, and tomorrow she is going to be induced. Sitting down at a table dressed in a red tablecloth which hangs almost to the floor, in the centre of the restaurant, surrounded by candles, I look at Amy in the glow of the little flames.

We reach across the table and hold hands over our menus which lie open and unread. Her eyes are bright, her smile young, her dark hair shining in waves around her face which still, after fourteen years, holds me entranced – every freckle and line, a face I have seen from teenage years to now. A face I have seen torn to agony and despair, and a face I have seen and kissed in moments of bliss and desperation. I am still learning so much about her.

This may be the last night when it's just us, I say.

I know, she says, placing her left foot on mine underneath the table, a ritual of closeness we have performed ever since I can remember. It makes me feel good. We are so caught up in the moment that we don't notice the waiter looming above us, impatient to take our order. Amy isn't so hungry so we share a meal: lasagne, followed by chocolate ice cream.

The year before Elowen was born I ran a trail marathon – twenty-eight miles through forests and over hills. I burst into tears when I crossed the finishing line. But that feeling, which I thought was deep relief, hardly compares to how I feel now. This endless marathon. All that we have been through, are going through, charges between us in a wordless way.

The food arrives, breaking the spell of inseparability. We tuck in.

This is the best meal I've ever had, I say.

You always say that, Amy says, smiling. *Look at us,* she says. *Look at us here in this restaurant. I can't believe we've made it.*

That night, unable to sleep, while Amy lies on her side snoring beside me, my mind runs over the weeks since we got back from Nant Gwynant for another summer of waiting at Hope Cottage for our child's birth. I focus on these recent memories, as if cataloguing them will help me control this moment. I reach for my phone and begin scrolling back through photos of the summer, and when I can't find a photo to fill the gap, I put my phone on my chest and think of the times between them.

There was Amy's fall on a riverbank close to Hope Cottage, after which we drove straight to Southampton General (the first time we had been back to that hospital since Elowen's birth). Amy lay on the bed while a midwife checked her over with the Doppler machine, just as she had searched for Elowen's heartbeat. But Eli was fine. Amy was fine too, left shaken by the experience, as was I. After that, we decided it best to stay in the New Forest, to be nearer hospitals. More trips to Nant Gwynant would have to wait until after Eli was born. And so back in the New Forest, I finally finished my workshop. I also chainsawed and split a load of wood I had felled last year, stacking it high in the log shed that I always keep open for the swallows. Swallows that Elowen did not see, but Eli will.

Father's Day came round, during which Amy and I made a bonfire in the field. We burnt all the offcuts from my workshop build, mounted the fire high and threw on boxes we'd been storing from Elowen's pram and car seat, and when the rain fell we stayed outside until the flames spat and subsided into embers. We were also invited to Amy's friend's wedding, where there were people whom we hadn't seen since before Elowen, and some friends that had fallen away almost a year ago, after a few messages of sympathy. We went along just to prove to ourselves that we could do it, and how far we'd come – turning up and seeing familiar faces was not easy, but it was enough. Even now, when I am among people I find it hard to relate to them. I feel removed, not always lonely, but singled out. Amy feels this too. It's something we bring up in our counselling sessions: Elowen's death has removed us from our old selves. But I'm OK with that now. I have to be.

Elowen's first birthday pressed in on us in July: the twenty-seventh.

Not wanting to be at Hope Cottage that day, we took time away and stayed in Dorset at Amy's Dad's. We had the house to ourselves for a week. We brought the teddy bear, still filled with ashes. We were consumed by grief. *Where is our one-year-old girl? She should be here with us. I want to hold her and kiss her.* I remember us saying all this aloud to the Purbeck Hills, or as we sat close to one another in the evenings watching TV. As Amy was six months pregnant, she took it easy, taking gentle walks in the sun along the coast. We returned to Shell Bay, Studland, for the first time in almost a year.

I still think of that blissful day, when Elowen was on her way, and we lay in the sand all together, feeling happy. Going back, we swam in the sea again, and I talked to Eli underwater. While we were in Dorset, Amy decided to write down every detail of the days running up to and after Elowen's birth. She needed to do it, had to. Afterwards, we held onto one another just like we held onto one another when we got home from the hospital that Monday, and promised to love each other no matter what – if we had our love, even if there was nothing else, no one else, only us two, then that would be OK.

Our last day in Dorset was spent walking out to Swyre Head. By noon, the sun was bright and hot. House martins, sand martins, swallows, all flickering overhead. The sea was a haze of blue. We lay down together on the grass and fell asleep.

Back at Hope Cottage, during those summer evenings, Amy often felt the heat uncomfortable in her pregnancy, so we would go outside for fresh air and watch the wild ponies running across the forest heath, their hooves thudding the dry ground, manes billowing under the darkening sky. But after Elowen's birthday, I started to hear the nightjars returned to the heath. I turned away from them, closing the windows at night, not seeking out their calls as I did before. I sometimes wish they would go silent. Some days, I would hurl a stone at each one. And the blossoming heather brings me only terrible reminders, like that sprig of heather we placed in Elowen's coffin, with acorn from her oak. The heather, like the nightjars, are singing of her death. Will I ever be able listen to these creatures as I did before? Will I ever be able to see the summer colours of the heath with joy again?

If not for me, then for Eli? I think so. I feel that confidence building.

Tomorrow is going to change everything. Looking back, I see clearly how, in such a violent and sudden way, I lost the wild I once adored. I look at trees or animals or mountains now with such detachment. I no longer wish to hoard what I see. I don't have the appetite anymore. This is not to say I am disinterested or lack love for the natural world. It's just that, when I hold Amy, for instance, and she holds me back and I can feel her heartbeat, real and close, the warmth of her human form is more powerful. I think, naively, I thought nature cared about me somehow. But wildness, nature, whatever the hell we call it, will go on without us and doesn't care for the daughter we lost. So perhaps I am wiser. I do not depend on it, or expect it to be there for me. Because it isn't, and never was. I enter into the world now more soberly, with humility, perhaps because I am fearful. I have become acutely aware, at times overwhelmingly, that death is here, always. Nature is life. Nature is death. And because of my fear, I cannot judge or own what's outside of my thoughts and feelings. I cannot colour the landscape the way I want to. I am not the centre of gravity, because being alive has scared me shitless.

What stands out for me as I lie here in bed, the clock past 2 a.m., is the day when I made a point of revisiting the oak in the forest where I lit a fire in the run-up to Elowen's birth. Digging away the earth, I found the half-burnt logs, cindered and preserved. I took one back home to show Amy. I held it in my hands for a while, she held it too. I placed it carefully on a shelf in the living-room, and I look at it from time to time, thinking of how I felt back then, before Elowen, and who I am now without her, and with Eli on the way.

Eventually, I can feel the heaviness of sleep. I turn on my side with Amy facing me. She is sleeping at peace. I also see that she's left her earrings in from our evening date.

*

After almost a full twenty-four hours of induced labour, Eli is finally born by C-section at 11.30 a.m. It is October 10, 2018. At one point,

Amy is sent on a walk outside to help stir things into action, but because the weather is so sultry – an October heatwave – when she returns to the delivery room, Eli's heart rate rockets to dangerous levels, to the point that his vitals aren't being picked up at all. Amy is taken away for an emergency C-section, and time stops when he's pulled from her. There is a hush, which, for once, means the world has paused *for* us.

He is alive, and I bury my head into Amy's neck.

All that I have held back is released.

Eli is taken over to a table where he is warmed under a bright lamp and wrapped and rubbed in a soft white towel. I go to him – rush more like – and look into his dark, glistening eyes and stroke his soft head, and touch his warm body, and hold him. I take him over to see Amy who is lying down, a midwife beside her, the surgeon stitching her up, and place him in her arms.

Back in the hospital room, family hold him. My Dad. Mum. Amy's family. I hold Mum and Dad and Eli close to me, my arms around them all. A framed picture of Elowen is on a shelf beside Amy's hospital bed. We watch him open his eyes. He is warm, so warm. Nothing short of miraculous.

I tend to Amy over the few days that we stay in the hospital, helping her to her feet, easing her carefully back into the bed. Her C-section wound is incredibly tender. I help her go to the toilet and shower. I do all I can.

As Eli sleeps in a small, clear cot that is risen up as high as our bed, dressed in white with his pink, sleeveless arms down by his side, or swaddled in a blanket that was (is) Elowen's, we gaze at him. We watch his tiny chest rise and fall, rise and fall, and his head turn from side to side, his mouth quiver and yawn. So this is what it's like. This is what parents feel when they gaze at their living child. We are not afraid. I can hardly believe that he is alive, warm to my kiss, responsive.

Pulling up at home once back from the hospital, the sun out, the heatwave lingering on, trees beginning to show their first signs of autumn, we both hold the car seat – the very same car seat we bought for Elowen – and walk proudly through the front door.

*

I swaddle Eli, then lay him down carefully on the bed. Morning sunlight streams in, lighting up his face. He turns his head away. I scoop him up then lay him down again on a blanket which I fold, with Amy's help, around his body. He is wrapped in the blanket Amy and I bought from the Makah Reservation in Washington State.

I am going to take him outside. First, to the ash and oak at the far end of the field, and then down into the woods, to introduce him to the trees, and the trees to him. A small and necessary adventure. I want the outdoors to become a part of his daily routine, the feel of the forest air as familiar as the touch of milk on his lips. A part of his nourishment and care. I have been planning this moment since Elowen.

As I step outside into the autumn heat and cloudless sky which have lingered since Eli was born a few days ago, my grief is not confused. I anticipate that in times to come the grief will hit – I fear that my heart will still want Elowen, or that people will assume Amy and I are fixed now. The time Amy and I have spent over the past year, dedicating ourselves to one another and to Elowen, will this be squeezed out in the demanding whirl of nappies and sleepless nights?

For now, I think of nothing else but this moment with my son.

I am holding him, and I never thought I could love so much.

Amy closes the front door behind me and settles down on the sofa to rest. Out in the garden, Eli looks like Elowen. But he is not her. I look at him in the light. My boy, my son, my heart.

Daisy and Dilly run forth and then back beside me. Dilly's barking doesn't disturb him – it's a sound he knows from Amy's womb. He turns his head from side to side, agitated by the sunlight on his eyelids, which are almost see-through, paper-thin and lined with a delicate pattern of capillaries. I bring him round upon my other arm, out of the sun.

The ash tree is almost bare, the shadows of the branches cast down on us in strips and angles of darkness and light. The sun has risen over our home. I tilt my head back against the trunk, close my eyes, and almost fall asleep until Eli and I are both woken by Daisy and Dilly barking at a squirrel perched, cockily, on a fence post. It runs across the top rail, then leaps up over our head, claws its way up the ash, scuttles out along a branch, then leaps again onto another tree, then another, until out of sight. Eli murmurs. I fight the sleep from my eyes and take him further on.

We pass under the oak. There are slabs of concrete scattered on the ground, half buried in mud, trodden and pressed down by horses, vehicles, passers-by. These are the ones I smashed against the tree and the gate during the first days and nights at home without Elowen. I look at them for a while, and the fact that I'm holding Eli does nothing to assuage the memories of that night's tearful rage which, coming fast upon me now, set my heart thumping. But the rawness of the feeling wanes when I look back at Elowen's brother beneath the oak, with each leaf set out like a promise.

Further down the track, in the woods, the silver birches shine out through the darker tones and colours of the pines. Down here, it feels like summer. Eli, in his blanket bundle, is warm against me. Daisy and Dilly run ahead and turn right into the firs. Long shadows stretch across the mossy ground which is soft under foot. The sight of resin, crystallised white on a spruce tree, its aroma strengthening as I near it, brings a sense of routine comfort.

I lay Eli gently down on the mossy earth, letting his blanket fall open around him. His little face is golden in the sun. His eyes are closed. He is in a deep sleep. I lie down beside him, at first on my side, staring closely at his features, then lie on my back and look up into the evergreen canopy of the spruce trees.

Though these woods are only a five minute walk from home, getting here, feeling as I do now, has been an endurance. To say I am not tired out by everything would be a lie. I am here with my son – and I can say that with confidence – who is beginning to stir from his sleep, his mouth moving in the way that suggests he is hungry.

He begins to cry, his voice filling the forest, an infant voice I never imagined I would ever hear after Elowen.

I do still long to hear her voice.

My daughter in the woods, just like my dream of her saying my name in the sunlit clearing.

But my son is crying now, not erasing or overshadowing, not silencing her, but somehow sounding alongside her. He doesn't even know where he is, but I do. Scooping him up in both of my arms, I traipse back up to the cottage, and his cry is almost deafening as I walk into the house, where Amy is ready and waiting to feed him. There is still moss on the blanket as I fold it away into the cupboard.

Tonight, we will put him down to sleep in the cot that we assembled for Elowen. Perhaps I will read parts of a book that we bought for her. He will lie beside our bed. And when he stirs for food, we will take him, Amy and I, into Elowen's room and lie him on my chest, or on Amy's, in the tall blue rocking chair. Just above us, up on a shelf, are Elowen's footprints and handprints standing side by side with Eli's. I always wonder who got to spend time with her after we had left the hospital. Who pressed her little hands into the mould?

I miss you, Elowen.

And so tonight, outside, the owls will call. A badger or fox or roe deer will set off the outside light, but will disappear, as it always does, into the woods, or out onto the heath, before I have the chance to stand with Eli close to my chest and peer out into the night. After Eli's feed I will burp him, lay him down, then kiss, as gently as possible, the bridge of his nose, and breathe him in, filling my lungs with him just as I did with his sister.

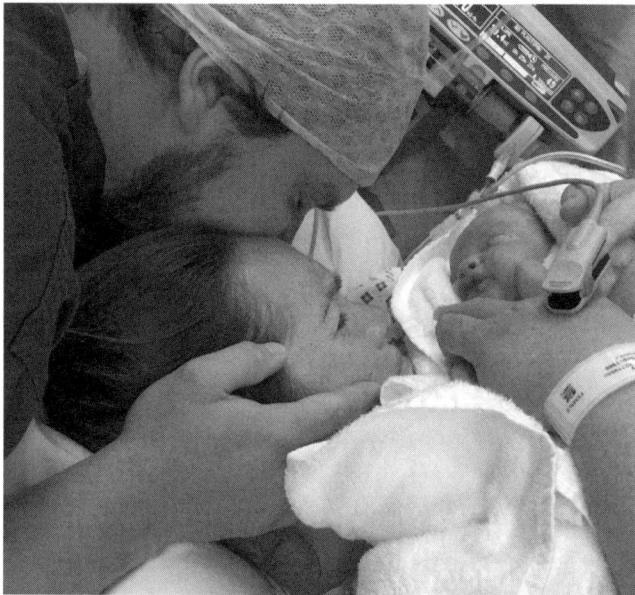

Afterword

A light snow has fallen in the night. There are white dustings on pale ice, in the hoof prints of wild ponies that lead down further into the forest, in dark ruts and hollows, in the cupped palms of dead oak leaves that litter the ground and break softly under foot.

All morning, an easterly has been blowing strong. The highest birch tops – sprays of bare branches against a cold, blue, February sky – lean and sway. I watch them for a little while.

Daisy and Dilly run and leap. Though they are older now, their age showing in Daisy's stiffened gate and in Dilly's white hairs around her eyes as she swings her head my way, they still show an undimmed spriteliness when out here.

Eli is with me, keeping close to my side. It's very cold. Refusing to wear gloves, his little hands are red. He gives them a puzzled look as though they do not belong to him. I teach him to tuck them into his jacket pockets, and he does so, obligingly, then totters on ahead of me, quite sure-footed and confident. He stops, looks around, looks up, craning his neck, unbalancing himself, almost tripping. He flings out his hands from his pockets, and arches down with determination to inspect the ground, searching for clues that explain why he nearly fell. *What tripped me?* I am in love with watching him. A sense of warmth comes over me, despite the bitter wind at my back, as I follow him through holly groves, birch trees, and on towards the biggest oaks that draw me on as much as I walk towards them.

We are stopped in our tracks by a solitary pony that passes in front.

Eli yells *neigh! neigh!* The pony walks on, taking no notice of us, except for a sideways glance of her eye.

Further into the forest, there is no snow on the ground. Although it does lie on the tops of the oak branches, lending a ghostly girth to their size. And when the sun shines on that snow, the branches wear a white bark of brilliance.

I crouch down behind the largest of the oaks, shielded from the wind. Eli joins me, but not too close. He yells *Daisy, Dilly!* at the top of his little lungs. They come running.

As I look at him, I am amazed that he's only two years and four months old – a measure of time spilling over with incalculable preciousness. Caught up as I am in the momentum of parenthood, a sense of time slowing rarely comes, but my eyes now open on my son in a frame of timelessness and stillness. I see him and am in awe of this beautiful person. Suddenly, the frame breaks. The stillness shakes and time resumes. He runs on, I follow him.

I find him standing beside a fallen beech that is green with moss and covered with a bright, thin coat of snow. Though we have been here before, I show him, first the root-plate, half-exposed and jutting out abruptly like a cob wall resurrected from the earth, then the yew tree that grows snug against the lower trunks of the beech, and the holly which has somehow managed to grow out from between them, and whose canopy mingles with that of the yew. I know this place well. A place of the heart. Three trees that hold a world of feeling.

Soon we will be moving from this place. The shadowy pain of living at Hope Cottage has not relented. We think a different direction may help. Not here, not Snowdonia. We are trusting our gut. And yet, although I know in my gut that the move will be good for us, I am finding it hard to admit that soon these woods, the heath, the sunsets and big skies – and more specifically Elowen's Oak and Eli's Oak – will be far away.

I must come back, often. I must. There has been so much change, upheaval. I am hoping that this next move will work out for the good. Eli is two now. Elowen is three. We are moving forward as a family.

While Eli busies himself investigating the roots of the beech that dangle out from the root-plate like old ropes and laces, and throws himself into the stack of leaves that have banked up against the beech tree (the crisp rattle of them as he tumbles), I take a moment to look around, listen to the wind overhead, and be still.

I feel tired, drained by the getting ready for the move.

A memory comes to me. No, this is stronger, more than a memory, an upsurge of images and feeling breaking through into the present. I see Amy, just over three years ago, towards the middle of July, in the run up to Elowen's birth. She is walking this way, slowly, breathing heavily in the summer heat. I am walking beside her. We have just done a long walk in the woods, the last long walk before Elowen's birth. We rest here before the final slog home. I jump up onto the fallen beech that is bright and green in the sunlight. As I walk up and down the tree, stopping at its base where the yew begins, I describe how I'm going to bring Elowen here, make a camp in the nook between the yew and the beech, set a candle in a low cavity in the holly tree. Amy is catching her breath while my excitement fills the hot, summer air. We are happy.

As I watch myself and Amy leave for home, the memory – again, the word memory is inadequate – subsides and I am back in the present with Eli, but still ringing with the same feelings as then. Time doesn't mean much to me anymore. Love and grief – well, love *is* grief – take me deeper than where structured time can feebly scratch. Time doesn't heal. Nature doesn't heal, though it has helped in so far as I have desired it to help. Nothing is healed. There is restlessness, integration, adaptation, accommodation. There is work, and we have worked hard. And there is love. A love as certain as death, as wild and difficult.

So here in the woods I am left saying to the space around me. *Elowen,* I say. *Where are you? I know you are here, and not here...*

Eli is trying to climb up onto the beech tree, while at the same time sticking out his tongue and sampling the snow. I walk over to him, smiling. I lift him up onto the tree and hold his hand. As he carefully walks along the fallen tree, his little feet in their yellow boots make perfect footprints in the snow. At the point where he is too high for me to keep holding his hand, almost out of reach, I lift him off and set him down on the ground.

I imagine someone here when we are gone, on their walk in the woods, stopping by this beech tree. They will see a set of small footprints that suggests a child walked up and along the tree, and then simply disappeared.

For some reason I turn around, feeling that I'm being watched. My heart races, thumping in my chest. I close my eyes and hold out my hands. A wind, a long rustle of leaves.

Eventually, it's time to get home, to finish packing. So, with Elowen beside me, and Eli up on my shoulders, I leave the woods.

Amy is already by the door, waiting for us. She is smiling. We make quite a family.

Acknowledgements

This book should never have been written. My daughter should be alive now, six years old on July 27th 2023, running, playing, doing all the things a six year girl should be doing. I knew, however, that even in those first months of losing her, I was going to write about her and our story. I had to do it.

My first deep thanks go to Bren, our grief counsellor at the Firgrove Centre, without whom I don't think I would have been able to write this book. She guided us to a place where we built the strength to say Elowen's name out loud – just as any parent should. As always, love and gratitude go to supportive family and friends. And, more generally, thanks go to those that have asked about her name, or at least tried, no matter how fumbling.

Thanks to my agent, Matthew Marland at RCW, who was determined to find the book it's right home. Receiving feedback from big publishers such as 'there's no market for grieving male', and 'this book is too sad to edit', didn't waver his unfailing belief in the book, and the timely importance of its story. I am so glad, then, that it eventually found its way into the caring hands of Little Toller. I cannot say enough about how supportive and generous and kind they have been. Thank you.

W. S.

Gooseham, Cornwall, 2023